Mathematics with Reason

*The Emergent Approach
to Primary Maths*

Edited by

Sue Atkinson

Heinemann

PORTSMOUTH, NH

This book is dedicated to the memory of Yvonne Ward, Oxfordshire Adviser.

HEINEMANN EDUCATIONAL BOOKS, INC.
361 Hanover Street
Portsmouth Nh 03801-3959

First published in 1992 by
Hodder & Stoughton Ltd
Mill Road
Dunton Green
Sevenokas
Kent
England

First published in The United States in 1992 by Heinemann.

ISBN 0-435-08333-3

Editorial matter copyright and chapters 1, 2, 3, 7, 11, 14, 15, 16, 17, 20, 23, 24, 25, 26, 28 © 1991 Sue Atkinson; chapters 4 and 6 © 1991 Sue Atkinson and Shirley Clarke; chapters 5 and 18 © 1991 Shirley Clarke; chapter 8 © 1991 Sarah Killworth, Lesley Neilson and Sue Atkinson; chapter 9 © 1991 Sue Gifford; chapter 10 © 1991 Alison Base; chapters 12 and 27 © 1991 Marion Bird; chapter 13 © 1991 Sue Atkinson and Alison Base; chapter 19 © 1991 Sue Atkinson and Moira Proudfoot; chapter 21 © 1991 Owen Tregaskis; chapter 22 © 1991 Nick James.

Typeset by Taurus Graphics, Abingdon, Oxon.
Printed in Great Britain for the educational publishing division of Hodder & Stoughton Ltd, Mill Road, Dunton Green, Sevenoaks, Kent by Thomson Litho Ltd

Contents

About the editor

SUE ATKINSON is a primary teacher, primary maths consultant, and tutor for the Open University. She is engaged in research in primary maths curriculum development and has recently become a part-time lecturer at Westminster College, Oxford.

About the contributors

ALISON BASE was, at the time of writing, a teacher at Dr. South's Primary School, Islip, Oxfordshire. She is now deputy head at Garsington Primary, Oxfordshire and was a member of the PrIME team.

MARION BIRD is senior lecturer in maths education at West Sussex Institute of Education. She has taught across the age range of 5–18 years and has written widely on maths education.

SHIRLEY CLARKE works at the Institute of Education as inset coordinator for assessment. She was formerly a primary teacher and primary maths consultant in the Inner London Education Authority. She has worked extensively in a range of primary classrooms.

SUE GIFFORD is senior lecturer in maths education at the Roehampton Institute, London, and has worked in a variety of London Schools as a teacher and maths consultant.

NICK JAMES is involved in running in-service maths education for teachers in South Africa. He was formerly a teacher and maths advisory teacher, then lecturer in maths education at the Open University.

SARAH KILLWORTH was, at the time of writing, nursery teacher at New Hinksey First School, where she worked with nursery nurse, Elizabeth Stone. She is now headteacher at Headington Nursery School, Oxford.

LESLEY NEILSON is the nursery teacher at West Oxford Primary School where she works with nursery nurses Carol Adams, Lin Byrne and Janet Hemming.

MOIRA PROUDFOOT is a headteacher in Oxfordshire with a full-time teaching commitment. She was a member of the Oxfordshire PrIME team.

OWEN TREGASKIS is a teacher who worked with primary aged children for 20 years. For the last 8 years he has also worked with students in training and teachers on in-service courses at Cheltenham and Gloucester College of Higher Education. His main interest is in the development of children's mathematical thinking.

Foreword

In reality, no one can *teach* mathematics. Effective teachers are those who can stimulate students to *learn* mathematics. Educational research offers compelling evidence that students learn mathematics well only when they *construct* their own mathematical learning. (National Research Council, 1989, p. 58) The implications of this statement are clear. We, as teachers, must find ways to help children construct their own mathematical understandings. We need to provide children with experiences that will help them carry out the construction efficiently and with mathematically accurate results. *Mathematics with Reason* relates the experiences of several British teachers as they searched for such teaching ideas. The book is written in a style that makes it easy to relate to your own classroom. It includes descriptions of children's investigations and reactions that will remind you of children you have taught, while suggesting things you may like to try.

The *Curriculum and Evaluation Standards for School Mathematics* states that children should: 'value mathematics, be confident about their ability to do mathematics, be problem solvers, be able to communicate about mathematics, and be able to reason mathematically' (NCTM, 1989, pp. 5–6). The teaching ideas and guiding principles set forth in *Mathematics with Reason* will help you provide instruction that is in keeping with these goals. A good example is the list found in the conclusion to chapter 7; it suggests fundamental teaching ideas which, as the author says, 'unlock children's own intuitive methods . . . then they can operate at full power.'

In discussing grades K-4, the *Standards* also suggest that 'it takes careful planning to create a curriculum that capitalizes on children's intuitive insights and language in selecting and teaching mathematical ideas and skills. It is clear that children's intellectual, social, and emotional development should guide the overall goals for learning mathematics' (p. 16). *Mathematics with Reason* clearly achieves these goals. It does so through interesting accounts of children's reactions to specific teaching and learning experiences and through suggestions growing out of the children's responses.

The teaching approaches described here will make children feel that they are in control of the mathematics rather than the mathematics being in control of them, both during instruction and later, when the mathematics is put to use in real situations. It is especially pleasant to experience so many good ideas about teaching while reading accounts of how children have reacted and what they have said in particular learning situations. It is wise to base what we do on a firm research foundation, but putting the evidence and suggestions into a context with real children makes this book particularly enjoyable, and valuable, reading.

Thomas E. Rowan,
Elementary Mathematics Consultant

References:
National Council of Teachers of Mathematics, 1989. Curriculum and Evaluation Standards for School Mathematics, Reston, Va.: National Council of Teachers of Mathematics.
National Research Council, 1989. *Everybody Counts: A Report to the Nation on the Future of Mathematics Education.* Washington, D.C.: National Academy Press.

Editor's Preface

Why do people find maths so difficult? Why does it cause such panic? Why do some teachers lack confidence when teaching maths? How is it that a child can spend a term learning multiplication tables, but then be unable to see how that knowledge will help to find the cost of buying 50 cream eggs?

This book explores some of the thinking processes underlying such questions. It looks at ways of making our maths teaching more effective both at home and in school, particularly in the light of the requirements of the National Curriculum. I hope that it will be used as a resource book for dipping into, for home, classroom, and for discussion starters for in-service work.

The book has been divided into three sections: Section A, the Introduction, considers the theory; Section B includes teachers' real-life stories of how *Mathematics with Reason* works in practice; and Section C looks at the practicalities and the different ways forward.

To help those who want to follow through certain ideas, there is a heading at the start of each chapter, within Section B, indicating the themes it contains, the age group of the children etc.

Most of the work described has arisen from teaching and advisory work, and from research. Any apparent emphasis on subtraction and place value is because these became a focus of my own research, and does not indicate any belief in their particular importance. The rest of the work has arisen from discussions with groups of teachers and parents, from in-service days, and from various primary teachers' support groups.

Throughout this book we have referred to he and she, but both of these terms should be taken to apply to both sexes. We have tried to avoid the clumsy wording of 'he/she', 'him/her', 'himself/herself' etc.

Acknowledgments

The author and publishers would like to thank Joy Dunn for providing the cartoons on section pages 55 and 150. Hodder & Stoughton have made every effort to trace copyright holders for all previously published copyright material, and believes it has done so, but if copyright holders wish to contact Hodder & Stoughton they should do so at the publishers address.

Sue Gifford wishes to acknowledge the help of Shirley Clarke, Valerie Heal, Christine Pugh and Razia Begum for chapter 9.

I am grateful to the teachers and parents from in-service days, the support groups I run for primary teachers, and the many other people who have contributed to this book. I especially want to thank Shirley Clarke for her advice on the typescript – and hours on the telephone! Nick James, John Mason, Owen Tregaskis, Martin Hughes, Tina Bruce, David Fielker, Gillian Johnson, Pam Atkins, Jan Tugwood, Joy Dunn and Chris Laybourn have all helped at various stages, though I take responsibility for the final product. Several other colleagues have contributed to the book, but prefer not to be named. Thanks also to my colleagues in the Oxfordshire PrIME team, to Adrian Townsend for his support and encouragement, to David Atkinson for his help and advice, and to Wilma Rawson for that wonderful moment in my classroom when the initial idea for this book was born. Also to Kathy Havekin of Hodder and Stoughton who has been a marvellous editor. Most of all I am grateful to all the children, teachers and parents with whom I have worked in the classroom, including those from: Drayton Primary School, Oxfordshire, especially Marian Whiting and Pauline Higgs; New Hinksey First School, Oxford, especially Jackie Nauman, Margaret Tatton, Jean King, and Adrian Townsend; West Oxford Primary School, Oxford, especially Bobbie Jones and Jack Smellie; Brington Primary School, Huntingdon; Grendon County Combined School, Buckinghamshire; Weald Middle School, Harrow, Middlesex. They have been a constant source of delight and inspiration.

Sue Atkinson
January 1991

Section A   Introduction

— 1 — Children as mathematicians
Sue Atkinson

> THEMES: background theory; links with apprenticeship reading and developmental writing; the term 'maths with reason'; why maths is treated differently

A significant feature of current primary education is the growing trend towards building on the skills developed from the children's home-learning which they bring with them to school. This is reflected in the way the National Curriculum non-statutory guidance in both English and maths advocates an emphasis on the children's own methods.

One of the assumptions of this book is that educational practice which starts from where children are, (what they are thinking and the skills they already possess etc.) will be the most effective means of teaching new concepts, mathematical or otherwise. This practice will build on children's intuitive beliefs, strengths, and their 'home' or 'informal' language. This kind of educational practice will, we argue, enable children to progress more rapidly through the levels and attainment targets of the National Curriculum.

Whereas earlier educational psychologists, following Piaget, argued that children have severe developmental limitations in the their understanding (and in some senses of course that cannot be disputed), working with children can take on a whole new perspective if one builds on the modern theories of child development. These focus on the *meaning* and the *strengths* that the children already have.

The work of Margaret Donaldson (1978), Martin Hughes (1986), Vygotski (1983), and others, shows how much children are capable of. If we can negotiate shared meanings and strive to unlock children's attempts to communicate with us, (rather than interpret what they do exclusively in adult terms), we become aware of their enormous potential. There is considerable evidence (Wells and Nicholls, 1985; Donaldson *et al* 1983, and others) that by involving children actively in the processes of their own education, enabling them to search for personal meaning in what they *can* do, we deepen their understanding and open new doors in their learning.

Developmental writing

This attempt to build on what children already know underlies the emphasis on 'developmental' writing described in the work of Marie Clay (1975); Donald Graves (1983); the SCDC National Writing Project; and Nigel Hall (1989). This change in emphasis has borne fruit. In classrooms where developmental writing is encouraged, children write much more and much earlier in their school life and, it would seem, with much more meaning, involvement, enjoyment and artistic expression than was previously thought possible (Nigel Hall, 1989).

The aims of the National Writing Project include: valuing children's own work; making use of all the real writing opportunities that exist (such as thank you letters, notes, diaries etc.); providing a variety of pens, paper, and other writing equipment; providing a role model, by the teacher writing for herself; valuing writing by 'publishing' it, so viewing children as writers; and ensuring that the purposes of the writing is clear to the child.

The apprenticeship approach to reading

Similar thinking underlies the 'apprenticeship approach' to reading developed by Liz Waterland in her book *Read With Me*(1985). The adult provides the role model, reading *with* the child, as well as the child spending time in the classroom reading her own book. The literature available to the children is 'real' in the sense that they are encouraged to 'read' books which are published because of their literary merit, and not, for example, because of their 'structured' vocabulary or phonics.

In schools where delightful picture books lure children into the world of story and dominate the reading corner, reading is much more important *to the children*. It becomes more fun and the focus of much of the classroom activity. Books have a meaning that children can identify with – there is a reason for reading.

A balanced approach

Of course, many teachers believe that there is no one correct way to teach reading and writing. They still keep the more structured 'reading books' for use with children who need support. In writing, most teachers would want to give children as many different experiences as possible to encourage different sorts of writing. Teachers continue writing for children, as they have done for years, providing children with a model to copy.

In any 'new' thinking, teachers select ways to teach their class from ideas around them, but they are often caught between conflicting claims of researchers. Some would argue, for example, that the developmental approach to language is not working and that standards are falling, whereas others are convinced of its effectiveness. Somewhere down the middle is the teacher trying to teach her children in the most effective way.

Why treat maths differently from language?

In primary schools where there is ample evidence of 'good practice' in language work, why is it that maths is so often the poor relation – often a solitary activity, based on a closely followed scheme, workbook, or an ancient set of workcards? A group of teachers gave the following reasons for treating maths differently.

- Teachers perceive themselves as poor mathematicians.
- Teachers lack confidence and therefore over-rely on a maths scheme for security.
- School policy requires a scheme to be followed.
- To cover the requirements of the National Curriculum children need to be 'pushed on' and a scheme achieves that.
- Parents have been taught by teachers that maths is rows of 'sums' all ticked (in red!).
- Teachers are willing to try out new ideas but continue to believe that 'real' maths comes out of a text book.
- Use of a text book can control children very effectively and in a class of thirty, when the teacher is working with four children, the need to get twenty-six occupied means that the maths scheme often saves the day.
- Teachers and children have a very limited view of what maths is.
- Children are viewed as having potential for language activities, i.e. they come to school with abilities that are nurtured and developed. By the age of five, children have about half of the adult spoken vocabulary, but almost no maths *of the type that is normally measured and regarded as 'school' maths.*
- Children are viewed as empty vessels when it comes to understanding maths concepts. Teachers see their role as emptying the jug of knowledge about maths into the children.
- The maths in construction, design, science, technology, PE, printing, cooking, woodwork, the home corner, etc., is not recognised as such and so is not developed in any depth as a significant and meaningful mathematical activity.
- Maths *is* different! Much of it is abstract, and this sets it apart from many other aspects of the curriculum.

A 'developmental' or 'apprenticeship' approach to maths?

Is there a developmental approach to the learning of maths corresponding to that in language? It seems much harder to find developmental maths in primary classrooms than developmental language teaching. But we hope to show in this book that such an approach to maths is not only possible but effective. We have tried to answer the following questions:

- What would developmental maths mean in theory, and in the practice of implementing the National Curriculum?

- What can we translate from the apprenticeship approach to language into the maths curriculum?

- What is needed by teachers to help them allow children develop the intuitive mathematical skills and concepts that they already have?

Releasing potential

This book is about releasing potential – both the children's and the teacher's. It is about encouraging teachers (however nervous they are about teaching maths) to experiment, to view maths from a different standpoint, to take a step back and let the children try to do it their way – a way that shows there is a reason for maths.

So we argue that there can be a developmental approach to maths though we recognise that more research is needed. We also believe that many of the aims of the National Writing Project apply equally in the context of maths. The contributors to this book are *not* advocating one correct way to teach maths. We argue for a balanced approach to maths teaching, incorporating the very best of current good primary practice, and relating this to the requirements of the National Curriculum.

Despite the differences between language and maths, we will show that there are considerable similarities in the thinking processes involved. So for teachers who are confident in language teaching, much of the way they teach language can be directly applicable to the teaching of maths. The 'apprenticeship' approach to maths, for example, would involve the teacher doing some of her own maths – organising timetables, lists, charts, etc. – in the classroom, where she can share her work with the children. She will also join in with the children's work, so that adult and child are learners together.

What shall we call this approach to maths?

We face a difficulty in deciding what this approach to maths should be called.

- *Practical maths* This does not say enough. Just because children are using apparatus, does not necessarily mean that the activity is meaningful and relevant to them.

- *Emergent maths* A good term, implying children emerging as mathematicians. We maintain in this book that children come to school mathematically able – it is 'school maths' that can breed the panic. However, the term 'emergent' may have taken on a special meaning in writing terms, so 'emergent maths' does not quite express what we mean.

- *Developmental maths* This is also a good term, but has the problem that it could give the impression that mathematical understanding *always* goes through certain stages, This may be true, but more research is needed on this.

- *Constructivist maths* This is another good term. Constructivists believe that children must have the opportunity to construct meaning for themselves. However, it could give the impression (*a*) that children must, therefore, construct *all* meaning for themselves – which is not what we mean. The parent and teacher play a vital role in that construction – the role of the sensitive intervener who often supplies language and gently guides the child towards expressing the concept in a meaningful (but not necessarily conventional) way; or (*b*) that maths is rather like the progressivism of the 1960s and 1970s when teachers were led to believe that the teacher just stood back and let it all happen.

- *Intelligent maths* (Richard Skemp) Yes, this conveys much of what we mean. Intelligent learning is understood and therefore remembered. It has meaning for the child. But we also want to convey some sense of the emergence of children as mathematicians, implying a developmental process.

As a result, we have chosen the term 'maths with reason' as a summary term which seems to convey what is most helpful in these other terms.

What is 'maths with reason'?

Maths with reason rests on exactly the same philosophy of child development and classroom practice as developmental writing and apprenticeship reading. What we mean will emerge throughout the book where it will be seen that maths with reason includes the following features:

- It is maths which starts from the secure 'home learning' established in the child before she comes to school.

- It is maths based on understanding.

- It is a balanced approach using both traditional and new methods.

- It builds on the child's 'home' language and gradually, and with great care, introduces the more formal and special language of maths.

- It has as its overall aim 'to develop a positive attitude to maths and an awareness of its power to communicate and explain.'

- It puts great emphasis on the child's own methods for calculating and solving problems and rejects the previous practice of heavy emphasis on standard written algorithms.

- Maths is regarded as a powerful tool for interpreting the world and therefore should ideally be rooted in real experience across the whole curriculum. Maths with reason becomes a part of the classroom dialogue; a way of explaining the world of the child with all its mysteries and wonder.

- Maths with reason is rooted in *action*– learning through *doing*. So schemes of work (the translating of policies into actual classroom practice) always start with *activity*.

- Maths with reason puts less emphasis on representing numbers on paper as 'sums' and more emphasis on developing *mental images* in the child, and it is through language and emphasis on the inter-relationship of language and action that these mental images are used as a bridge towards the mastery of the codes of maths – its specialised symbols and meanings.

- The main tool for child and teacher to employ in the mastery of maths concepts is *language*, not pencil and paper exercises from text books. The child is encouraged to *talk* about what she is doing and the teacher's craft is to bring all her knowledge and skill into play to make her intervention appropriate.

- Errors are accepted as an essential part of the learning process. They enable teachers to assess what meaning the child is making of the activity and often become a starting point for discussion. The child, freed from the fear of criticism, will more readily experiment with ideas and mathematical language. He will think aloud, and in so doing will release enormous creative potential into the group.

- Teachers and parents work on the maths *they* are doing *with* the child. Mathematical activities like cooking, shopping, gardening, the family budget, estimating how much food is needed for the meal, are all shared with the child. In classrooms, teachers make their problems explicit to the children e.g. how shall we organise our assembly?

- Maths is brought out of the child's everyday situations, e.g. playing ludo or chess, sharing biscuits, deciding what is fair, whose turn it is on the computer and how many more days to go until someone's birthday.

- So, maths with reason emphasises the thinking processes of maths, and these are made explicit in the conversations between adult and child. The focus is on the children doing their own thinking – which is valued by the teacher – not on the children trying to work out what is in the teacher's mind.

In other words, maths with reason is consistent with other 'good practice' in primary education. We believe that it leads to higher attainment in maths in National Curriculum terms, and helps children to become mathematicians.

Martin Hughes (1986) made clear that a crucial element in maths teaching is that children come to school with considerable mathematical abilities. In the next chapter we outline his work which underpins the rest of the book.

—2— A new approach to maths
Sue Atkinson

THEMES: the work of Martin Hughes; background theory; the problem of children's poor maths attainment; children's own methods and symbols; the challenge to teachers and parents

One of the key recent books about maths education is *Children and Number* by Martin Hughes. His research indicates possible ways of improving children's' performance in maths – an area of great concern to teachers and parents. This chapter only presents Hughes' main findings as they relate to maths with reason, and readers are strongly encouraged to read *Children and Number* for themselves.

What is the problem?

Many surveys show that children can lack basic mathematical understanding in practical situations. Hughes looks at this problem in relation to number with some surprising conclusions.

The standard of maths seems poor in many children.

Hughes finds that young children do, in fact, have considerable mathematical language and understanding before they come to school. We will call this their 'home' or 'informal' language and understanding, because it uses the everyday informal language of the home and the child's familiar world.

One of Hughes' main points is that the more formal language of school maths (both as spoken at school and in written standard symbols, e.g. 2 + 2 = 4) is very different from this informal 'home' language. *It may be that the gap between these two languages holds the key to why so many children perform so poorly in maths tests.*

This is obviously a vitally important piece of research for parents and teachers because it involves both the home and the school, and one of Hughes' conclusions is that parents and teachers should try to work more closely together.

Central to Hughes' argument is the belief that the ability to solve problems is at the heart of maths. This is a major theme in the Cockroft Report (DES, 1982 para.249) and in the National Curriculum. In other words, teachers should be aiming to teach not only concepts and skills, but also how to apply concepts in practical situations as it is here that children seem to fail in tests.

Hughes set out to answer why it is that surveys point out the shortcomings in children's understanding of practical applications of maths, and why this kind of mathematical understanding, (often called problem solving) is so difficult for so many children.

Piaget in proportion

Piaget's work has been, and still is, of enormous significance in influencing ideas about how children learn. His theories rest on the idea of discrete stages of cognitive development in the child, i.e. separate stages that the child has to go through. Piaget was led to conclude, for example, that children under seven years of age are incapable of logical thought and are able only to see things from their own perspective.

Hughes argues that there is evidence to suggest that this view of young children – as very limited and illogical thinkers – is not correct. He suggests, as do other psychologists, that these apparent limitations to children's thinking can be partially explained because Piaget set up such unreal research situations, and used such complex language that the children simply did not understand the context and the meaning of the task that Piaget was setting them. In other words, the thinking required for the task was what Margaret Donaldson, in *Children's Minds*, calls 'disembedded thinking'.

If, however, children are set tasks similar to those used by Piaget, but in a context familiar and meaningful to the child (a task with 'human sense'), it can be shown that children understand far more than Piaget suggests. As well as his own work on this point (McGarrigle, Grieve and Hughes, 1978), Hughes cites the work of Donaldson (1978) and Gelman and Gillistel, (1978). The importance of this for teachers is the change in emphasis. Piaget focused on what children *do not* know whereas Hughes focuses on what they *do* know. This has important consequences for what we teach, and how we teach it.

Hughes proposes an approach to maths based on these new ideas of how children seem to learn and it is this new approach which underlies *Maths with Reason*.

What do children know before they come to school?

Hughes found that children know a great deal about number before they come to school. He found that even three-year-olds can carry out simple addition and subtraction provided the problems were presented in a context which made 'human sense' to them, and provided also that the numbers were kept small. Hughes describes a number of games that he devised to play with children in which he explored this pre-school ability. One of these games, the tins game, is described a little later on. These games can provide an interesting starting point for parents and nursery reception teachers.

A paradox

Having found that many children know a great deal about number before they come to school and that they seem at this stage to display a surprising range of mathematical abilities, Hughes focuses on an intriguing problem: '. . . we have something of a paradox: young children appear to start school with more mathematical knowledge than has hitherto been thought. In that case, why should they experience such difficulty with school mathematics?' (Hughes 1986b, p. 36).

School maths language is like a foreign language to the children and often fails to integrate with their already accomplished mathematical 'home' language.

The language of school maths

Children's impressive array of mathematical abilities does not always seem to carry over into the classroom because of their difficulties of learning '. . . to translate between their concrete understanding of number and the written symbolism of arithmetic.' (Hughes 1986b, p. 53). So, although children arrive at school often able to perform calculations such as 'what is two bricks and one more brick?', most teachers of small children wisely hesitate about using the written formal code $2 + 1 = ?$. Likewise a child who is asked 'How many is three and one more?', might say 'One more what?' because it makes no 'human sense'. But, ask the same child 'How many is three bricks and one brick?' and he will answer 'four' because he can understand the problem as it refers to bricks.

This difficulty in translating the concrete understanding of number into school maths language is delightfully illustrated in the following conversation between Martin Hughes and Patrick (aged four years, one month).

MH: How many is two and one more?
Patrick: Four.
MH: Well, how many is two *lollipops* and one more?
Patrick: Three.
MH: How many is two *elephants* and one more?
Patrick: Three.
MH: How many is two *Giraffes* and one more?
Patrick: Three.
HM: So how many is two and one more?
Patrick: (*Looking Hughes straight in the eye*) Six.

(Hughes, 1986a, and Hughes, 1986b p. 47.)

The problem with school maths language is that it is often about nothing in particular i.e. 'What is two and one more?' – 'One more what?'; it is new to the children; it is difficult because it involves unfamiliar concepts; and, it uses words children already know in special ways such as 'and' (meaning 'add'), 'take away' (Chinese ?) and 'makes'.

So, if the maths itself is not presented in a way that is meaningful to children, if it fails to make 'human sense', and if unfamiliar language is used, problems will almost inevitably arise.

Children's own methods

Using fingers for counting

Hughes recommends that some difficulties could perhaps be prevented if children were encouraged to use their own methods from the start.

For many children, counting on fingers is their favourite 'own method'. Many parents and teachers try to discourage children using fingers for calculating, but Hughes points out how important their use is for children.

The gap

What seems to happen with many children is that they develop a completely separate way of thinking about the maths they do at school, because it fails to integrate with their accomplished informal 'home' mathematical language.

One feature of this gap is the way that children are often observed to be splitting thinking and understanding from calculations they perform. Both teachers and parents frequently see this happening when children do a calculation and come up with an answer that a moment's thought would show to be ridiculous. An example of this splitting of reason from calculating could be where ten-year-old children calculate how many 52-seater coaches would be needed to get everyone to the seaside. If, for example, 234 people were going, it would not be uncommon to get a response based on correct arithmetic (234 divided by 52), but devoid of reason – 'we need four-and-a-half coaches.'

How do we close the gap?

'Helping children to make these links is probably the single most important task in early mathematics education' (Martin Hughes)

Hughes suggests that we may be able to help children to make the crucial links between their own personal and meaningful maths with which they come to school, and the more formal and complex language of school maths, in very practical ways.

1 We could emphasise and encourage the use of the children's own methods of calculation.
2 Linked with this, we could encourage the children's own invented symbols that have meaning for them.
3 Teachers could find out all they can about the children's mathematical background from the parents, e.g. Do they like numbers and counting? Do they play mathematical games at home – dice or cards? Do they use a calculator or computer? Do they like and seem to understand activities that have a maths content, such as cooking, shopping, woodwork or using construction toys like Lego and Meccano?

4 We could set maths tasks in meaningful contexts, to allow for the children to make 'human sense' of the task and to allow them to be able to translate the unfamiliar maths language into their own individual understandings of maths.

Invented symbols

One of the most interesting aspects of Hughes' work is the invented symbolism which he found to be present in the young children he worked with.

The tins game
Hughes put out four identical tins with lids, each containing a different number of bricks, usually one, two and three bricks with one empty tin. He shuffled the tins around and asked each child individually to find, say, the tin with three bricks. Of course, this was guess work because all the tins looked the same. Once the children grasped the game, Hughes put labels on the tin, gave each child a pen and asked them to put something on the paper to show how many bricks were in the tin. The tins were shuffled after each child had written on the labels and Hughes then asked them to find, say, the tin with three bricks in. This time the children had their own invented symbols to help them. It turned out that their own representations were clearly meaningful to them and many children were able to identify correctly the number of bricks in the tins. (See Fig 2.1a and 2.1b).

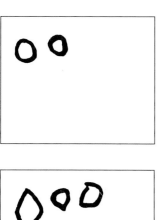

Figure 2.1a Representations of 1, 2, 3 and 0 bricks by Anna (4 yrs)

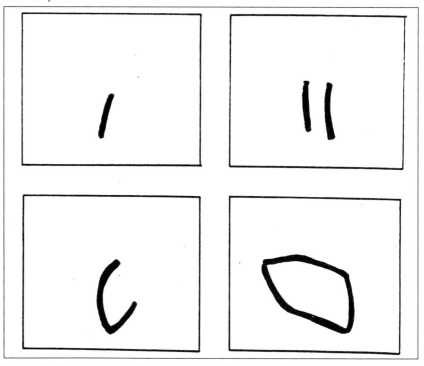

Figure 2.1b Representations of 1, 2, 3 and 0 bricks by Paul (3 yrs 8ths)

This tins game produced children's invented ways of recording numbers and some of the children's ideas are reproduced here. Again, readers are recommended to refer to Hughes' book, *Children and Number*, for greater detail.

There were various sorts of responses from the children when they were asked to 'put something on the paper'. Some children produced what can only be called 'scribble'. This doesn't, of course, mean that the scribble didn't have some meaning to the child, for as with early writing, it may well be that children have to go through this stage. Children are learning that print conveys meaning. Their 'scribble' is an attempt to say something in print and teachers are well aware of the confidence with which children 'read' these early attempts. Other children produced work that Hughes was able to analyse – shown below.

Alison (4yrs 2 mths) : 2 bricks

Leanne (4 yrs 3 mths) : 5 bricks

Halla (3 yrs 6 mths) : 1 brick

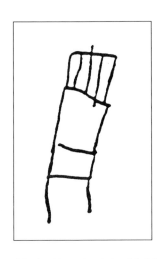

Figure 2.2 Examples of idiosyncractic responses

Nicola (4 yrs 4 mths) : 5 bricks

Analysing children's work

Hughes put the children's work into four groups, and readers may like to relate these types of responses to those found in the National Writing Project. He put the 'scribble', together with other representations where the children's meaning was not clear to him, in a group called 'idiosyncratic responses' (see Figure 2.2).

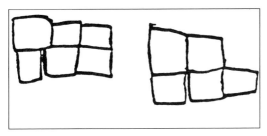

Daniel (5 yrs 11 mths) : freehand drawing representing 6 bricks and 5 bricks

Fig 2.3 Examples of pictographic responses

Rachel (4 yrs) draws round bricks

Other children produced work that was grouped as 'pictographic responses' because it showed some semblance to a picture of what was in front of them (see Figure 2.3).

'Iconic responses' were those that, like the pictographic responses, showed a one-to-one correspondence with the bricks (i.e. an attempt at the right number of bricks), but where the children made some mark rather than a picture – so for three bricks they did three tallies or three houses (see Figure 2.4).

Fig 2.4 Examples of iconic response

Mutale (4 yrs 3 mths) : 5 bricks

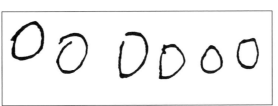

Emma(5 yrs 2 mths) : 6 bricks

Pamela(5 yrs 1 mth) : 3 bricks

'Symbolic responses' were those where some sort of conventional symbol was used (see Figure 2.5).

Neil(3 yrs 5 mths)

Leigh(6 yrs 11 mths)

Figure 2.5 Examples of symbolic responses (all representing 1, 2 and 3 bricks)

Kashif(7 yrs 4 mths)

From the diagram (Figure 2.6) it can be seen that it was not until children were about seven years old that conventional symbols became the most common response – a fact which surprises many adults.

Hughes notes several interesting points about these invented symbols, but just two will be mentioned here:

1 Children attached great meaning to their own symbols and they were able to interpret them up to a week later.

2 Very few of the children used conventional symbols, even children who were familiar with conventional number symbols.

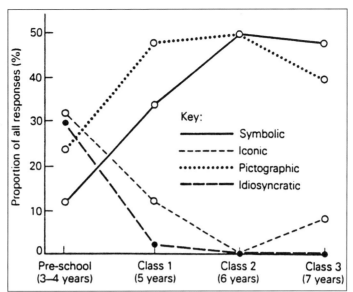

Figure 2.6 Type of response: variation with age

For teachers and parents the importance of invented symbols would seem to be:

- that it could show the apparent irrelevance of conventional symbols for very young children – which may reflect a similar irrelevance of, say, the traditional way of writing fractions, for an eight-year-old; and
- that it shows a clear link with early writing.

What conclusions can be drawn?

Hughes' work as it relates to maths with reason can be summarised as showing the following:

- Young children start school with their own understanding of maths and with a surprising range of mathematical abilities.

- These abilities are clear when children operate in concrete situations that make 'human sense' to them.

- When children are at school they often fail at mathematical problems where knowledge has to be applied.

- Maths should therefore have a purpose and meaning and make 'human sense' to the child.

- A gap seems to develop between the child's own informal and concrete understanding of maths and the language of maths as it is used in schools.

- Helping children to make the links between home and school maths is a <u>vital and important task for teachers and parents in the maths education of children.</u>

Challenges facing parents and teachers

While Hughes recognises that there is much more to be discovered about the ways children learn maths, the implications of his work for parents and teachers include the following:

- We need to redefine the aims and objectives of early maths education, giving the links *between* the concrete and the formal more emphasis.

- Parents and teachers need to work together to relate the child's 'home' mathematical background to the school's approach. For a more detailed account of this see p. 161.

- We need to build on the mathematical strategies which the child already possesses at the start of school, e.g. using fingers or counting up and down the number sequence. These are the maths strategies that are *meaningful* to young children.

- 'Obviously, we want children to move on eventually to new and more powerful strategies, but if these are forced upon children regardless of their own methods *they will not only fail to understand the new ones, but will feel ashamed and defensive about their own.*' (Hughes, 1986b, p. 177 – editor's emphasis).

- We must respect children's own invented symbolism. 'As with children's informal methods of calculation, their own invented symbolism must be given much greater prominence in the classroom.' (Hughes, 1986b p. 177).

- '. . . indeed, it turns out that *children's own inventive notations are likely to be far more appropriate in these early stages than the conventional symbolism of arithmetic . . .* Yet children are rarely encouraged to use these methods in school.' (Hughes, 1986b, p. 170 editor's emphasis)

- 'Whatever the source of children's translation difficulties might be, their consequences are undoubtedly profound. If children do not readily and fluently translate between different representations of mathematical problems, then a dangerous gap will develop. At best, this may simply mean that they will carry out their formal procedures competently but automatically, and with little understanding of their rationale or possible application. This would seem an accurate description of the way many children – and adults – perform arithmetic today. A much more damaging consequence is that their formal procedures will become faulty. Without any concrete underpinning, isolated mistakes can become habitual errors, and a *bizarre written arithmetic can easily result.*' (Hughes 1986b p. 171 – editor's emphasis).

- We should attempt to explain to the children the history and purpose of conventional symbolism. As Laurie Buxton (1982) says, 'The answer is not to avoid mathematical symbols in a child's earlier experience. Rather one should capitalise on situations where the children feel a need for symbols.' (It is interesting to relate this point to some of the aims and objectives of the National Writing Project; see p. 73.)

- We should take particular care when using symbols. In some maths schemes, non-standard symbolism (such as arrows) can be used to the point of confusion.

- We should always try to put maths into a context that children understand. For example, rather than using 'sums' out of context, we could try to set maths in 'real' or practical situations. Examples of teachers doing this can be found in Chapters 10, 16, 17, and 21.

- We should not be afraid of explicit teaching.

- We should recognise the value of computers and calculators. Teachers using LOGO find many benefits reaching right across the curriculum, but for the purposes of this book, the important points are that it stimulates mathematical discussion and thought, it improves language, communication and group cooperation generally, it engages the children's interest and develops concentration, and because of its problem–solving nature, it tends to integrate 'home' and 'school' maths, and gives a sense of purpose to the maths.

This chapter highlights the importance of building on children's strengths and making the appropriate links between 'home' and school maths. Teachers must make maths have meaning and a sense of purpose for the children – in other words, to give maths a reason.

The next five chapters give a practical focus of some of these theoretical themes.

We want to thank Martin Hughes and Basil Blackwell, publishers, for permission to reproduce diagrams and to quote from *Children and Number*.

—3— What makes successful problem–solving?
Sue Atkinson

> THEMES: *background theory; low achievement in maths; the problem with problems; classroom organisation; effective maths teaching*

A strange anomaly seems to emerge in maths lessons. On the one hand, we see children who are quite competent at computational skills go to pieces and are unable to manage when confronted with a page of problems, and on the other hand, we have frequently shown that 'problem–solving' is a major way in which children learn. What is going on here? Are 'problems' contexts in which children perform poorly or well? Why should it be that children *learn* best in problem situations, yet continue to *function* best when only straightforward and simple calculations are involved? The following examples may prove interesting:

Martin Hughes quotes this very illuminating example from Hart (1981) in which children aged eleven to thirteen were asked:

'The Green family have to drive 261 miles to get from London to Leeds. After driving 87 miles, they stop for lunch. How do you work out how far they still have to drive?

87×3 $261 + 87$ $87 + 261$ $261 - 87$

261×87 $261 - 87$ $87 - 261$ $87 + 174$

Despite the fact that the children only needed to select the calculation required, only 60 per cent of twelve-year-olds selected the correct answer (261 - 87).

Adults have problems too

It is not just children who have this problem. A BBC survey (1990) of 1000 people aged between twenty-one and sixty found that:

- More than one in ten adults could not cope with calculating how much a dozen 30p chocolate bars would cost and how much change they would get from £10.

- Forty per cent could not divide a £30.35 restaurant bill between five people.

- Nearly half could not work out 15 per cent VAT on £80.

The people were allowed to use calculators, the tests were done at home, and the tests were disguised and made as friendly as possible so that people would be at ease.

Elizabeth tries to do some problems

Here is the sort of example that teachers encounter frequently. Elizabeth, a bright child of ten, was working on subtraction in a scheme. She successfully completed three pages of straight 'sums'. She then turned over to a double page of similar sums, but embedded in words – what the scheme called a 'problems' page. Elizabeth could not cope with this and said that she did not know what to do. The teacher knew that Elizabeth approached other problem–solving situations positively and successfully, so what was so difficult to her about this page of written problems? It was not simply a matter of reading the problems, as she was a fluent reader. The teacher sat with Elizabeth and, taking the problems one at a time, tried to explore what the real meanings of the problems were – trying to get Elizabeth to see the 'human sense' in them. Eventually Elizabeth saw the meaning of each problem and worked it out correctly in her head. But then she asked, 'How do I write that down?' She seemed unable to relate what she could now see as the answer, to the conventional form of a standard algorithm. Elizabeth is by no means alone, and many teachers find this inconsistency in children's computational skills and applications required by 'problems'.

It would appear that Elizabeth needed both to have the problem explained in a context which was meaningful to her and, having got the right answers mentally, she still, despite being in the top maths group, needed these related to standard conventional ways of writing sums down.

Here, then, is a clue to understanding our anomaly. As Margaret Donaldson points out, (and we stress elsewhere in this book), a crucial factor in successful mathematics is the *context* in which the problem is set. This must be *clear and meaningful* and make 'human sense' to the child. This isn't always the case with scheme 'problems' pages. Not only do children not care how much the wood cost Mr Smith when he was making his garage, but not many of them can find the situation meaningful.

What might contribute to this 'problem with problems'?

'Problems' in books can cause reading difficulties for some children, but it is often more complex than this, because they can also cause difficulties for good readers as well. Perhaps it is the language of 'problems'. There is clearly a huge difference between children saying 'How much squash do you think we'll need for the party?' and the grand text book language of 'Thirty-two children decide to have a party. Each child will drink 230 ml of squash and . . . ' etc.

Children see text book 'problems' as 'word sums' and perceive them as being harder than straightforward calculations. Children seem to operate in 'school maths mode' when they see maths written down, and this is characterised by:

- leaving behind informal, secure, intuitive methods;

- the use of taught school methods for calculations (standard written algorithms) – if they can be remembered;

- an apparent inability to continue to ask if the answer is reasonable; and

- the willingness to believe that *it need have no meaning!*

Adult   Why did you put a little 'one' under the line?
Barry   That's what Mrs Smith does.
(aged 8)

Ben, aged 9, calculating 27 + 3 wrote:
$$\begin{array}{r} 27 \\ +3 \\ \hline 57 \end{array}$$

but mentally he worked it out to be 30.

Adult   So which is right?
Ben   They both are.
Adult   Can you explain that to me?
Ben   Well, sometimes that happens when you write it down.

How can we teach maths more effectively?

- We need to ensure that problems are set in meaningful contexts.

- Writing maths down (hence the need to use symbols), tends to make children and adults operate in 'school maths mode'.

- Symbols can be very powerful – but they cause their own difficulties.

- Written maths often causes people to abandon their more secure informal methods.

- Written maths often causes people to forget how to perform calculations.

So how can we make the best of problem pages in schemes and other resource books? Basically, we should aim to:

- give the children plenty of time;

- let them work in groups so that they can discuss;

- give the problem verbally where possible;

- make sure the children feel the problem is real enough to be worth solving!

- make sure the problems are interesting;

- explain that learning to think problems through and find a solution is an important part of the National Curriculum, and it is an important 'life skill' which children will need as adults; and

- ensure that, particularly for under-sevens, the problem makes 'human sense'.

—4— The use of standard notation
Sue Atkinson and Shirley Clarke

| *THEMES: when and how to introduce standard notation; children's own methods and symbols; successive shorthanding; discussion starters*

The following sections have been produced by groups of teachers. They are provided here as a basis for discussion for groups of parents and teachers.

What is standard notation?

Figure 4.1 shows a collection of all the maths symbols we could think of.

The advantages of symbols
- Symbols are part of the universal language of maths.
- They are time-saving.
- Using symbols correctly can give children a great sense of achievement.
- Getting children to use them impresses the parents!

The disadvantages of symbols
- They do tend to restrict children's methods.
- You need a good memory to remember them and to use them confidently.
- You also need to understand (*a*) the symbol; (*b*) the process; (*c*) its application.
- They can tend to give a sense of failure if they are not understood.
- They are too abstract for young children.
- Copied symbols from books can mislead parents over what their children can understand.

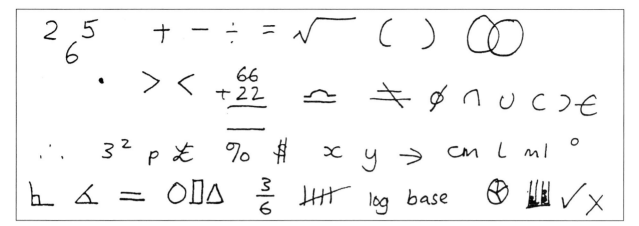

Figure 4.1 Standard notation

*Reasons for not
using standard notation*

- It may be the wrong moment for certain children. They may not be ready for anything other than their own methods which have meaning for them.

- They may not understand the need for any kind of quick shorthand.

- Someone else's method could cause some children to devalue their own methods causing low self-esteem and lack of confidence in maths.

- Standard teacher–taught methods can give an impression that it is the teacher who holds all the right answers and the power. This again can lower children's confidence and willingness to think for themselves and to produce their own methods.

- Some standard forms of notation and calculation are inefficient. For example, in many maths schemes, arrows are used in so many ways that children soon become confused.

*When are standard forms of
notation appropriate?*

- When the notation is understood.

- When the children understand the method being used.

- When the children have had opportunities to explore their own and others' methods.

- When it is the most efficient method for the children's purposes.

- When there is a 'democratic' atmosphere within the classroom.

*Why is it important to find
their own methods?*

- They involve children in their own learning, and therefore give children confidence.

- By comparing methods, children are helped to appreciate the need for using commonly understood symbols and for making their methods quick.

- It keeps open the idea of exploring alternatives, instead of the emphasis on 'one right way'.

- When children use their own methods, it is easier for teachers to be in touch with how children are thinking. The degree of abstraction that children have reached can be observed.

- Children's own methods and symbols are used and understood in writing, so the children can readily translate this into maths. This makes maths less of a mystery.

- Focusing on children's own methods increases the likelihood of building on the children's secure 'home' knowledge (see p. 44).

The process of successive shorthanding

When children work on 'do and talk' maths, first exploring mathematical ideas through games and activities, then recording in their own way perhaps with words and drawings, they are trying to represent the pictures in their minds. These pictures will often arise from the apparatus that the children have been using. The link can then be made from these pictures to standard notation. Children readily come to appreciate the need for increased speed of recording and the need to write things down concisely.

This is illustrated by work done by some seven-to-nine-year-olds on multiplication. Children first did several 'do and talk' maths activities, putting Unifix into groups, such as 3 groups of 4. They had to describe their work to each other, 'I've got 3 groups of 4 Unifix and it makes 12 altogether, 4, 8, 12.' Then the activity was made into games with two dice. When the children were confident with this (and had stopped putting out a 3 and a 4 for 3 groups of 4), they were asked to record their work in some way. Most drew the 3 groups of 4, and others recorded in longhand, writing 'three groups of four'.

They were then asked to find quicker ways to record this.

- Some children wrote 3 g of 4 (3 groups of 4).

- Others wrote 3 l of 4 (3 lots of 4).

- One group liked to write: 3 ④.

This last example was clearly quicker than using any letters, so the teacher encouraged these children to share their method with the rest of the class.

The teacher could see a clear link from this last method, with the 4 in a circle, to the conventional writing of 3 (4). The children just had to draw two of the sides of their circle. The teacher explained to the children that if they use this bracket symbol, every mathematician in the world would understand them. The children were very impressed.

Clearly lots of children knew the 'times' sign – '×' – so this was obviously discussed in the class. These children seemed to have no problem in relating their own shorthanding to conventional notations, especially when using a calculator. After half a term's topic on multiplication they seemed secure with the concepts involved.

It had been a very slow process to start off with. Some children and parents could not see why they did not just learn tables, but by the end of the half term, it was clear that the learning which had gone on was very secure. Children were then able to learn tables quickly by heart.

When and how do I introduce standard symbols?

The problems for teachers are *when* and *how* to introduce standard notation. Clearly we want children to use conventional forms fluently and with understanding. If children are encouraged to use their own symbols from the age of five, standard symbols can also be introduced alongside the children's own, but generally, and this is true for all ages, after children have had a chance to link the meaning embedded in the maths to their own intuitive understandings and mental images.

One major way to get children to appreciate the need for quicker or standard symbols is, after giving them time to explore their own methods, to talk about these methods and compare them with the efficiency of the different ways friends have recorded.

In classroom settings where an emphasis is given to the children's own recording, activities need to be developed which expose children to the standard symbols. Two examples are given below.

1 Using calculators

It is clear working with young children who are given free access to calculators, that they readily come to understand the symbols of the four rules for themselves. However, they need help to link the standard symbols with the many words often used in the language of maths, e.g. the multiplication sign means 'times', 'lots of ', 'sets of ', and so on.

2 Activities designed to teach standard symbols

The simple activity called 'trio-tricks' (Open University Development of Mathematical Thinking) can be used by children from about the age of six. The activity is a series of cards with words like 'altogether makes', 'add', 'difference between' and the standard symbols of '+' and '-'. The children select three related numbers, e.g. 4, 5, and 9, then take it in turns to make as many sentences as they can using just these three numbers, e.g. '9 is 5 more than 4'; '4 add 5 equals 9'; '4 and 5 altogether makes 9'; and '4 + 5 = 9'.

The children set out their cards, making their sentences by slotting words into homemade card 'pockets'. Blank card is provided for the children to write in any symbol or word not given.

A second set of cards and numbers relating multiplication to division, can be made for children from about the age of seven. Here the numbers would be 3, 4, and 12, and the sentences would be along the lines of: '3 sets of 4 makes 12' and so on.

Cards provided would include the standard symbols of brackets, multiplication etc., as well as words like 'lots of ', 'divided by' etc. To help children accept these symbols, they could be told the following:

- These are signs and symbols that the world recognises, just like the Russian, Urdu and English alphabets.

- Just as we needed to understand Kelly's shorthand:
  (d b 6, 3, 3)   meant for her 'The difference between 6 and 3 makes 3', so it must be clear what we mean, and that is why standard symbols have developed.

- These standard methods are not necessarily 'better' than the children's own, but they are used throughout the world so they are important to learn.

We would like to thank all the participating maths consultants, advisers and teachers on the course run at the Abbey Wood Maths Centre entitled 'Is there a link between developmental writing and children's recording of mathematics?'

—5— Children's graphical representations
Shirley Clarke

I *THEMES: children's own methods; links with children's writing*

My research with children seemed to point out four or five stages in recording information graphically:

I asked different children aged between four-and seven-years-old, at many different times, to collect information about something they were interested in. When this had been collected they had, in most cases, produced a list of some kind. My next question was always 'Can you show clearly what you have found out, so that we don't have to look all down the list?' It became evident that the children's earliest graphical representation within this context tended to be a picture of each item arranged at random on the paper, e.g., for colours of cars, they would draw the following:

Figure 5.1

If asked to show more clearly which colour was the most popular (or how to make the information even clearer) strategies adopted included (*a*) drawing the whole thing twice the size! or (*b*) drawing (if it were the red cars) the red cars bigger than the others, or maybe just one of them.

The next 'stage' in evidence was the same drawings of objects but with set rings drawn around each group, as shown on the next page (Fig 5.2):

Figure 5.2

Figure 5.3

When asked to show more clearly which group had most, the strategies adopted included (a) drawing a thick line around the set ring enclosing the largest group; or (b) using some kind of visual aid to draw attention to the largest set (e.g. sun spikes, a tick).

The next 'stage' was the absence of set rings, still drawn objects, but arranged horizontally in a vertical column, in no particular numerical order, and with no one-to-one correspondence within the vertical columns (Fig 5.3).

The next 'stages' were more predictable. The horizontal arrays in 'stacks' appear to be natural for children for a considerable time. This is interesting compared to a conventional graph or bar chart which has vertical columns. Research from the 'CAN' (Calculator Aware Number) project also produced evidence that children write their own algorithms horizontally, rather than in a 'sum' layout and appear to develop a mental model of a linear number line, if standard methods are not given. Presumably, these 'horizontal' recordings reflect the directionality of reading and writing in which children are heavily immersed during the early years. Two questions which occurred to me at the time were (a) Is it educationally appropriate to present a sum or standard algorithm to children? If not, when should they be presented? and (b) Why is the process of children finding their own methods important?

I used a specific example of work I had done with two four-year-olds to help teachers see how best to encourage children to record their findings. The problem was as follows: 'The cook is cooking eggs and chips for dinner. She can only put six things on the plate: any amount of eggs or chips, but only six altogether.' The children were given one cardboard plate and lots of cut-out eggs and chips. After they had set up lots of combinations, I asked how we could remember all the ways to tell the cook. Figure 5.4 shows Martyn's first recording. The first plate drawn was the largest, a common start. He then realised the plates would not all fit if he carried on with that size, so they became smaller. In Figure 5.5 he decided to start again and, interestingly, started with six chips and worked round in a backwards spiral. In Figure 5.6 Martyn

Figure 5.4

Figure 5.5

Figure 5.6

spontaneously wrote the numbers underneath each plate to show the combinations. I had asked him if he could write on the paper what was on the plates, expecting him to write something simple like 'These are all the ways you can have egg and chips'. I was really surprised that he had written the numbers, and thought that this was an example of how, as teachers, we often have rather low expectations. This is one reason why I always try to ask open-ended questions. By asking Martyn to respond in this open-ended manner, he wrote the number combinations in this systematic way. Martyn's teacher was astonished, saying she did not know he could write the numbers, let alone make the addition bonds for six.

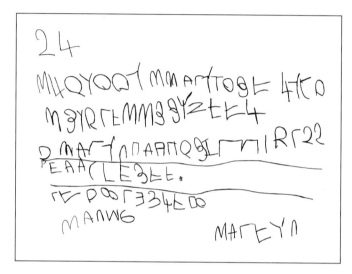

Figure 5.7

I then asked Martyn to write down everything that he did (Figure 5.7). He read this to me, and part of it was something like '4 and 2 together make 6'. You can clearly see the word 'together' towards the end of the top line. Then I asked him 'What were you actually doing?' and he wrote the bottom line 'MANW6' and read this as 'Making up numbers with 6'. This is a typical written response of a child of this age using the first letters to stand for words, but it is far from the typical sort of mathematical response we have come to expect from a four-year-old.

The addition symbol '+' is often omitted by children of all ages when left to record in their own way, as demonstrated by Hughes (1986) and by the findings of the CAN curriculum project (1991). However, the child working with Martyn did choose to use '+' when she recorded what they had done. This is included in Sue Gifford's article on p. 73, Figure 9.16.

— 6 — Children's own mathematical representations
Sue Atkinson & Shirley Clarke

| THEMES: children's own methods and symbols; successive shorthanding; recording maths; discussion starters

Questions for teachers

Working with groups of teachers we set about asking ourselves the questions we wanted to answer.

- Are we giving the children a sufficiently good role model in maths?
- Do we share our own maths with children?
- Do we join in maths activities, doing our own recording, and not just remaining an observer?
- Could we find maths activities where a more apprenticeship approach to maths could be used?
- Do we value the children's own work?
- Do children come into recording maths at a later stage than they do in writing, or are we just not seeing children's early maths because we fail to provide the opportunity?
- Where do maths and language separate – if at all?
- Is there a 'scribble' stage in early maths as with early writing? If so, how do we enable children to experience that stage?

Implications for teachers of children's own recording

As teachers, we sometimes assume children understand more than they do, so their own recording can be helpful in telling us what they really understand. Teachers need to provide challenging activities in order to encourage children to record their work in individualised ways, and they need to balance their own input and intervention with plenty of listening and observing.

They must be ready for children to come up with ideas that they would not themselves have thought of; teachers are co-learners, not the ones with all the answers. Working as co-learner seems to prevent 'learned helplessness' becoming a feature of the class – where the children learn to let the teacher do all the thinking. The teacher must work to promote an ethos within the classroom of mutual support and trust, where everyone's efforts are valued.

Teachers' reasons why children are helped by recording maths

- To communicate information.
- To remember things, results or numbers.
- To clarify a thought process.
- Because the teacher says so.
- To gain peer group admiration.
- To help work something out.
- To play or for pleasure.
- To compare methods.

Teachers' reasons why they are helped by children recording

- To help assess the children's understanding and stage of development.
- To help know what to plan next.
- To help children solve problems for themselves.
- To encourage children to compare methods.
- To keep children quiet and occupied.
- To extend a practical activity, especially when the teacher has to move to another group.

Parents' reasons for children recording maths

- To see where the child is.
- To be able to talk to the child about what they have done.

A summary of our main findings

- Children's own symbols hold enormous meaning for them. For example, invented symbols for price labels in the class shop, introduced and interpreted by a child, can be accepted and understood by the class for several weeks.

- Martin Hughes found that few children use conventional symbols for number operations. I have found this to be true, but recently I have found that children do sometimes spontaneously use standard signs and I wonder whether this is the influence of using calculators.

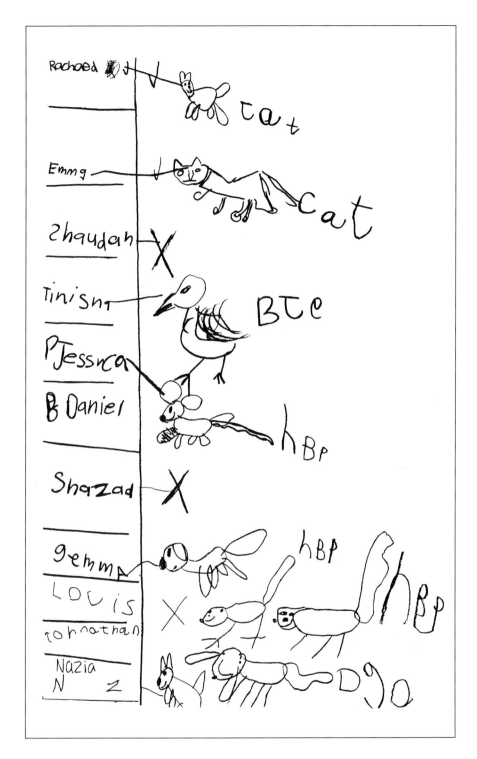

Figure 6.1

- Giving children of seven and eight years of age the time and space to develop their own symbols and shorthands for such aspects of maths, such as division and fractions, seems to reap benefits in secure learning. Most have few difficulties making the transition to conventional symbols when they feel confident and secure with the concepts involved.

- The processes of successive shorthanding provide a link between the language of maths and conventional symbols.

- The calculator seems to promote rapid understanding of conventional symbols

- A survey in many classrooms reveals that teachers prefer vertical columns in bar charts, but children prefer horizontal arrays, as noted by Shirley Clarke on p. 36. Children's organisation of their work does seem to depend, though on how they start their work. Children will mostly start off working horizontally, for both charts or writing. So, if the first thing they do is to list, say, favourite types of breakfast cereal, they may do this along the bottom of their paper horizontally, therefore leaving them to record their results vertically in stacks above this. If, however, they write down the children's names first, they are often influenced by the class register format, and so produce their list vertically, thus recording their results in horizontal arrays (Figure 6.1 on the previous page).

- Many children seem to have their own clear mental images for representations of maths, e.g. a personal number line. There is clearly a great significance in this for children's own recording.

- Many teachers report that when children see a need to record for themselves, the recordings usually help the children's thinking processes. However they report some confusion in thinking when recording is for another (usually adult) reason.

There is more research needed on these and other aspects of children's own recording, but my work so far shows this whole area to be a fruitful one for trying to understand more clearly how children learn maths.

—7— The power of children's own intuitive methods
Sue Atkinson

| THEMES: *maths thinking processes; children's mistakes*

I first became interested in children's own methods in maths after doing the Open University course 'The Development of Mathematical Thinking'. Then Martin Hughes published *Children and Number* and it seemed both Hughes and the views expressed on the course were saying something similar, i.e. children run into difficulties with maths, and attain at lower levels than we might expect, because adults impose their methods of working – standard algorithms – onto children.

Hughes suggests that children seem to develop a gap in their understanding in maths. I visualised this as a gap between two brick walls (see Figure 7.1). Ground level represents starting school. Children come to school with the secure foundations of early mathematical experiences which are part of 'home' language and learning (see Tizard and Hughes, 1984). This is part of the secure brick wall on the left. Children are receptive to new knowledge but, because teachers often fail to relate maths lessons to the foundation of 'home' understandings, another wall is built quite separately. This second wall – we will call it 'school maths' – has no secure foundation. It is based on teacher-imposed ideas and methods and, as I will go on to illustrate, this is the mode of maths in which children often seem to operate when in classroom settings.

Which wall am I building?

A reception class teacher making the context of the maths clear to the children would place a brick on the first wall, on top of the secure foundation – so 'two Unifix and two more Unifix' would make 'human sense' to the child. However, using unrelated 'sums' with unfamiliar symbols, like 2 + 2 = 4, then rushing on to 'tens and units' taught by a standard teacher-imposed method, would be in great danger of building on the unrelated and insecure second wall - where the knowledge could

43

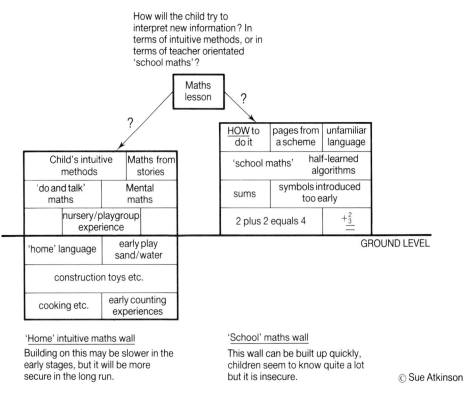

How will the child try to interpret new information? In terms of intuitive methods, or in terms of teacher orientated 'school maths'?

| Maths lesson | ? |

?

Child's intuitive methods	Maths from stories
'do and talk' maths	Mental maths
nursery/playgroup experience	

HOW to do it	pages from a scheme	unfamiliar language
'school maths'	half-learned algorithms	
sums	symbols introduced too early	
2 plus 2 equals 4	$+\frac{2}{3}$

'home' language	early play sand/water
construction toys etc.	
cooking etc.	early counting experiences

GROUND LEVEL

'Home' intuitive maths wall
Building on this may be slower in the early stages, but it will be more secure in the long run.

'School' maths wall
This wall can be built up quickly, children seem to know quite a lot but it is insecure.

© Sue Atkinson

Figure 7.1 The two brick walls

be worse than useless to the child, perhaps resulting in the 'bizarre written arithmetic' observed by Hughes (1986b).

The question I asked myself was that if Hughes was right, where were the children in my class putting their learning in any particular maths lesson? Was it being added to the secure wall, or was I using unfamiliar language or concepts so that it was being put, unhelpfully, on the insecure 'school maths' wall? (Hopefully, in time, the bricks from the 'school maths' wall can be built onto the secure 'home' maths wall, for eventually the meaning of '2 + 2 = 4' becomes clear, and children learn to use conventional symbols. The real power of maths comes in this ultimate combination of the power of children's own reasoning and the ability of conventional symbolism to communicate highly complex ideas).

I needed to look very closely at my own teaching, and even more at children's own methods of working. I set about keeping a diary of my work with children, and some of my results are shown in this chapter.

The classroom setting

I started a new full-time job as deputy head and maths co-ordinator in a big city first school. I was interested to discover that my six-to-nine year olds perceived 'real maths' as 'doing their scheme'. Although many of the children said that they liked 'doing sums', there was also evidence of considerable unease about maths. Comments such as 'it's hard', 'I don't understand it', and 'I'm no good at maths' were common. Maths was defined as 'doing the card' and when I tried to develop ideas or deal with difficulties, I got the reaction, 'But I've done that card'. My carefully thought out 'do and talk' maths activities, separate from the scheme, were not regarded as 'real' maths!

The scheme seemed to give some limited security to the children – and also to the teachers. Having a scheme certainly helped me to cope with those 34 six-to nine- year-olds, with their huge spread of ability! However, it was increasingly clear that the security the scheme gave was an unreal one. As I got children to talk about what they were doing, and as I probed into their understanding, it was clear that the scheme was failing. It was failing to give children confidence in what they were doing. It was failing to give them deep understanding or an adequate language of maths.

My initial questions

I wanted to tackle the problem of the children's lack of confidence and understanding. I wondered if I could focus them away from the obsession with getting the right answer and the related belief that the answer is the only important thing about maths. That is not to say that answers are not important – but I wanted to give equal weight to *how* you get the answer.

I set out to record my observations, and to look at children's own methods, taking as my base-line the fact that this class of six- to nine-year-olds had pretty negative feelings about maths and that I had taken as one of my assumptions that it was best to aim for understanding. I asked myself some questions. Was it really true that understanding was important? Would Martin Hughes' findings relate to my situation? What did the children in the class *actually do* when they engaged in mathematical activity? How is it that they pick up such a fear of maths? How do children *learn* mathematical concepts? Will letting them develop their own methods really help them to be better mathematically? My aim was to find out how they could learn maths in a more secure way.

How do children learn maths?

Filling in the dinner slip with the numbers of children having lunch, or sandwiches, or going home, was a daily task in which I involved the children. They were used to this, but totally thrown by my question 'How did you work that out, Andrew?

They found it hard at first to express their methods, but given encouragement, they would come up with explanations like the following. For example, given the problem: There are 31 children here, no-one goes home, 24 have sandwiches, so how many have school lunch? the children might suggest:

24 count on to 31 (usually using fingers);
31 count back to 24;
31 round down to 30, 4 from 10 is 16, add 1 makes 7;
30 to 25 is 5, so 30 to 24 is 6, so 31 to 24 is 7.

There was great surprise that there were so many ways to do it and the children gradually gained confidence in talking through what they were thinking.

One day, early in the school year, there were 30 children present with 25 having sandwiches. Several children said that they 'just knew' that left five to have dinner. This was something new. They really did not need to have a method in their heads for this as they knew their number bonds so well. Discussing this with the children, I found myself making it explicit that learning number bonds was an important aim in maths. This was received with great excitement by the children. As the weeks went by I began to see what was underlying that excitement. It was a sense of 'ownership'. I learnt that explaining *why* we were doing a particular piece of maths dramatically changed the attitude that the children had to maths.

The children appreciated being involved in why they did maths, and what it was all for. Was this something to do with Hughes' 'meaning'? It seemed that they were becoming more aware of their own mathematical thinking processes as their own methods were being emphasised and praised. They clearly found this exciting, and would frequently discuss the relative merits of different methods. The parents, too, became fascinated by the shift in emphasis in the children's perceptions of maths. Parents would tell sad stories of their own maths learning, and were delighted that their children were picking up a more positive message.

I was beginning to see that my early attempts at making children aware of their own thinking powers in maths was producing very positive results. Involving children in their own evaluations of their work seemed to have a similar encouraging effect. I obtained such dramatically positive results with my classes over three years that I have gone on exploring this issue in the past three years as a supply teacher in many different situations.

Unlocking children's own mathematical thinking

If we are teaching for attainment in National Curriculum terms, I conclude from my work over the past six years that children who are encouraged to use their own methods attain higher levels than children who are taught standard written algorithms first.

With this in mind, I will now explain how I try to get the children I meet in various supply teaching situations to unlock their mathematical thinking – to become aware of the methods that they use. In 'brick wall' terms, I am trying to create situations in which the children will develop an awareness of their own intuitive methods, and start to be able to place their school maths knowledge upon that secure wall which enables them to achieve at higher levels.

1 First I make them feel good about their own methods. 'Wow! What a good method Ross, could you explain it again?'

2 I make it explicit that *there is no 'right' way.* Everyone's method is

subject to checking of course, but if a method does not work, or a slip is made, *it does not matter at this stage – we are exploring ideas.* 'Don't worry that it didn't work out, Lee, you have some really good ideas.' (I am not saying that it is not important to get the right answer – but there is a big difference between making a 'slip' and a child being unable to see *how* to work it out. The difference needs to be made explicit. A slip can be corrected in a matter of seconds – not seeing how may take weeks of work.)

3 Minimising peer negative attitudes and derisory comments is often the hardest part. In supply teaching situations I find children very willing to offer information that they feel I should know, such as 'He won't be able to do it, Miss, he's thick', or they will roar with laughter at a child struggling to verbalise her method. How can freedom of thought survive if one is put down or laughed at?

4 Simply counting the number of different ways the group can find to work out one specific calculation encourages thinking.

5 I encourage the children to develop 'mental images' – 'pictures' in their minds. Some find this difficult, but children, and adults, *do have mental images.* Ask any group of people a complex (particularly spatial) question and you will often see them shut their eyes, or roll them up to the ceiling. Are they looking for the pictures in their mind? I think they are. Ask yourself the following question and see if you look for mental images. If you strung a cube up horizontally and dipped it into a bowl of water, it would not be hard to see that the shape at water level would be a square. However, if you strung the cube up by one of its corners and lowered it into the water, what would the shape at water level be then?

    A key theme to this book is the need to develop children's mental pictures of maths and I find, when working with groups in this way, that many children are able to describe their mental images.

It is important to work on classroom strategies to develop children's mental pictures of maths.

Drawing mental images

Recently, I spent ten minutes with a group of nine- to eleven-year-olds exploring how we worked out mathematical calculations mentally and talking about pictures in our minds. Then I set the quite difficult task of asking the children to draw (or write) about their mental pictures. Here is the sequence of my work.

1 I started with an easy calculation, 13 + 13. Most children were able to explain how they did this. Many worked out 10 + 10, then 3 + 3. Some did the tens first, some did the units. Some did 13 + 10 = 23, + 3 = 26.

2 Then another similar one, 21 + 24. I made it explicit that it was *how* they did it that I was interested in and that no calling out the answer was allowed as it would disturb other people's thinking. Any method was allowed, including using fingers.

3 I then moved on to subtraction, starting again with an easy one, $27 - 4$. Most counted back, some said 4 count on 3 is 7 so it is 23.

4 At this point I introduced the idea of pictures in their minds. Some children completely flipped out at this point – quite a normal reaction to a new idea. It is well worth spending time to let children talk about these ideas as this will help children who are not conscious of their own methods or images to begin to see what it is all about. Some people see a number line, some see Dienes blocks, and some see little tallies, or fingers. Whatever you see, it is OK.

5 Then I moved on to the harder subtractions which really test out children's security with their own methods. The sum $23 - 17$ led to the following different methods:

Yasmeen: $23 - 10 - 7 = 6$.

Kim: 17 add 6 is 23.

David: 17 count on 6 is 23 (done on his fingers and he insisted this was different from Kim's method of adding 'because it's a take away not an add').

Ross: 17 is 20 minus 3, and 3 and 3 is 6.

Alison: 20 take 10, plus 3 minus 7 makes 6.

Shakoar: 23 count back 7 is 16 minus 10 is 6.

6 This had all taken just a few minutes and I then explained that I wanted them to find a way to draw what they had in their minds – to find a way of making a picture to show what they do to work out a calculation. Of course, this is very hard for children, so talking about the pictures in their minds first is vital. Then everyone has some idea of what is expected of them. I suggest to children that if they are stuck, they could work with a favourite piece of apparatus, like Unifix or Dienes – *not* calculators yet.

It is really quite difficult to give children the security that they need to do a task like this, while encouraging them to explore their own ideas. Give them too much guidance and they will grab onto one of your ideas thinking that the task is to work out what the teacher has in her mind. Give them too little support and encouragement and they will panic and learn that maths is difficult to understand, the very opposite of your intentions.

7 Making all this a pleasurable and understandable task is vital.

Children's written work

Once the children began to write things down, 'gaps' started to appear between their own powerful mental methods and what they had become used to as 'school maths'. Some of the children's work is reproduced in Figure 7.2. Matthew, working out $16 + 17$ said, using his fingers, '16 (*pointing to one finger*), 17 (*pointing to the next one so that now he had two fingers*). It's 2'.

Gordon was totally unable to put on paper what he could explain to me. This raises important points – these methods are *mental methods* and children find it hard to relate them to written methods; and representing what is in your mind on paper is hard!

Gordon said to me, working out 121 − 49, 'Well, if it was 50, and if it was 120, it would be . . . (*mumbled and counted on fingers, touching his lips as he counted*) er . . . 50, 60, 70, 80, 90, 100, 110, 120 . . . so that's 80 (*holding up 8 fingers*) but it was 121, so add 1 . . . er . . . 81, but it was 49 not 50, so it's 82.' He remained unaware of his counting error, starting at 50, not at 60, but his method was rather good, and when I asked him to work out similar calculations mentally, he used his intuitive method correctly. However, a glimpse in Gordon's maths exercise book shows me that he could not work out standard written algorithms of similar difficulty. This seems to show that children like Gordon have developed their own effective mental methods, (on the secure brick wall), but his school maths has developed in a separate compartment.

Ross attempted to work out 63 − 47 by writing it vertically as in his scheme. I had written it horizontally on the board, but nine children wrote it vertically. All nine children got it wrong, for various reasons, Ross making a common error.

Was the problem too unrelated to anything else for him to give it any meaning? Did he know a bit about the 'trick' for subtraction? I asked Ross to calculate some other similar subtractions mentally, e.g. 71 subtract 38, 94 take away 27. He got *all* of these right! Clearly there was something about writing it down that caused him problems. I asked him to talk me through what he had done in his written work. He seemed unable to see his error. I asked him how he could check to see if his answer, 24, was right. He said, 'I didn't know how to do that'. Yet, when I challenged him to prove that his mental method was right, he had no problem explaining how he had arrived at answers *and* how he could check them. These are startling anomalies.

Figure 7.2 (here and following pages.)
Matthew (9 yrs)

$16 + 17 = 2$

Gordon (9 yrs)

$121 - 49 =$

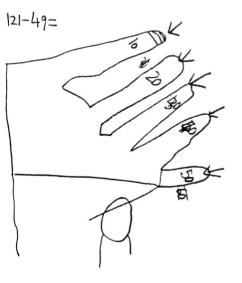

Ross (9 yrs)
Ross was able to work it out mentally,
but not on paper

$63 - 47$

$$\begin{array}{r} 47 \\ -63 \\ \hline 24 \end{array}$$

I took the 3 away from the 7 even and I got the for and Then I Looked at the 4 and the 6 I new that you could not take 6 away from 4 so I took 4 away from six

Katie's work is typical of many children. She sees it in words, not pictures. (The importance of language and the limitations of symbols are explored elsewhere in the book.) However, I would expect children like Katie eventually to find that they do have 'pictures' in their minds, and discovering these gives them enormous pleasure.

Annie had used Dienes apparatus to help her as she was stuck for almost 20 minutes on representing '23 take away 17'. Mentally she had no problem with this. She had told me she did it by adding on 6; yet she tried to show taking away 6. It is interesting that in order to represent it she came to me repeatedly to ask what to do next. It was quite hard to keep throwing the ball back in her court! She seemed to be one of those children who believe that a war of attrition can eventually get the teacher to reveal 'the answer' out of sheer frustration! Yet I was trying to give her a positive experience of maths! Was the task just too difficult for her – an example of mismatch? But her maths book showed she tackled this type of calculation regularly from the scheme.

I suggested crossing out to another child, and Annie then crossed out some of hers. I asked her if there was some way she could show what was left – the 'answer'. She couldn't. She eventually copied another child by putting a line around it. This method did not have much meaning for Annie! It is significant that when we were working verbally, all together, she was always one of the first to put up her hand.

Sally seemed to find the task of drawing her mental pictures easy and she represented her method with dots. She asked for something harder,

121 −49

go to the nearest ten (50) back that away from 121 wich ecuels
50 then ade 21 wich ecuels
    100
71 back the 1 away and the
answer is 70

Katie (9 yrs)

Annie (10 yrs)

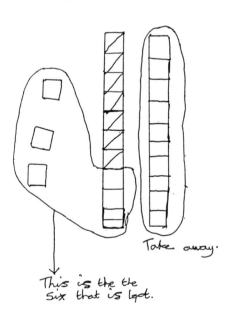

Take away.

This is the the
six that is lost.

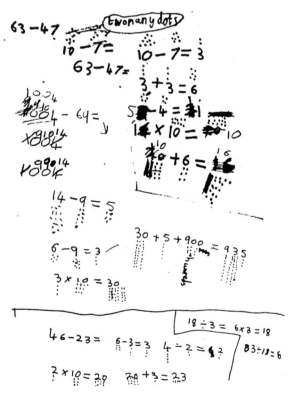

Sally (10 yrs)

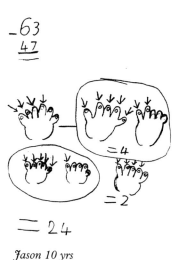

Jason 10 yrs

so I suggested that she try 1004 subtract 69. She managed this after a few false starts. I'm not sure that the dots are really one of her own informal methods. I think they may have been put in to meet my criterion of a 'picture'.

Jason insisted he had no picture in his mind (quite a common reaction in the early stages). He said he always used his fingers. Could he draw the fingers he was using, I asked? A look of relief came over his face and he sat down and spent 30 minutes counting on his fingers, drawing, rubbing out, and looking increasingly perplexed. At last he looked pleased with himself and I sat beside him. He explained his work, but unfortunately I had nothing to write on so the reasoning behind it (which sounded very plausible at the time), is lost.

It is worth pondering his drawing. *Top drawing* – is it 4 fingers take away 7 leaves 4? Or is it 7 take away 3, (which he has not included in the drawing) leaves 4. *Lower drawing* – is it 6 fingers take away 4 leaves 2? (This time working from left to right.) Whatever he meant he got it wrong, but it is very important to note that Jason did not have such problems with mental calculations of similar difficulty. Is there something about the calculation being written down?

I found that no child got 121 subtract 49 right, and wondered whether if I had written it vertically (as it was in their scheme) I would have got a different result?

Of course, some of the children were able to get the calculations correct, especially when they worked on them mentally, but there was a steep decline in correct calculations once they worked on paper. In this account I cannot adequately represent the powerful mental methods that the children shared when we worked together initially. These were often not related to these later 'pictures'. The children seemed to operate in a different mode once they had to write maths down. I call this 'school maths mode' and believe it to be the way that the insecure 'school maths' wall shows itself.

Of course, as a supply teacher I was having to pluck problems out of the air, and there were presumably difficulties for the children in understanding exactly what it was that a teacher they had known only for a few days was asking them to do. However, despite these problems, my account is presented here because I suggest that this sort of activity – making children's own methods explicit to them – is valuable and raises important issues. It helps teachers to see how their children are thinking so they can assess what each child needs next; and it helps to close up the gap that develops unhelpfully between the methods developed in school or shown to them by parents, and the intuitive methods that children have developed for themselves.

Why was so much written work wrong?

What was so remarkable in the work with the children was their enthusiasm as I praised and encouraged their mental methods and the speed with which they could mentally calculate accurately and confidently. This changed dramatically when writing down calculations of similar difficulty. These were often totally wrong, and children showed a marked resistance to applying their strong mental methods to the written work – for example their inability to check their work. This is a common reaction, but, given time and the opportunity to explore their own methods, the gap begins to close. Children begin to relate 'school maths' methods to their own methods.

Specific teaching

It also needs to be said that the importance of children's own methods does not eliminate the need to engage in specific teaching, particularly when children are experiencing difficulty. There *is* a place in maths teaching for exposition by the teacher, explaining what standard symbols, like + or - or = mean. It is a difficult aspect of our craft knowledge to know *when* and *how* to do specific teaching – and important to remember that we teachers tend to do far too much exposition!

When children seem to be struggling we apply our complex craft knowledge in exactly the same way as we do in language teaching. We do a great deal of observation, making formative assessments of what children can do and what they find difficult. We have to look back at the early ideas and concepts – the foundations of the brick wall – and ask ourselves if children are trying to build 'school maths' apart from their 'home' experiences. The activity described earlier, developing mental pictures, is one way to start to close that gap.

'Specific' teaching might be used to sort out *how* and *when* to teach standard notation and symbols; to work out what to do with children whose own methods have shortcomings, such as very slow, long-winded methods; and to help children who are persistently 'stuck' – one strategy being to let them choose someone else's method, or some piece of apparatus, and to go for understanding of just one way of doing it, repeating this until they succeed (unless there is a mismatch between the task and the child's mental abilities, when it is best to leave it and come back to it in a few months).

NB it is of course essential to involve parents with a child who is persistently stuck over the same thing, as your combined efforts will certainly be more successful than just one of you working with the child.

Conclusions

1 The main thing that I have learnt from this work is that it is important not to start with an adult-imposed method for doing a calculation, i.e. a standard written algorithm. The difficulty that many adults find with this is that it goes against everything that they can remember about

their own maths learning. We were shown *how* to subtract, *how* to do long division, *how* to operate xs and ys, and if in doubt we had little tricks like, 'turn it upside down and multiply'.

2 There is no one right way to teach anyone to do a calculation, but building the school maths onto already existing secure home knowledge seems to make sense.

3 It is a common finding in present day maths education, and implicit in the 1978 HMI report, that children who spend less time on arithmetic and more time engaging in a wider curriculum are the ones who actually achieve better. I have found this to be true over and over again with my own classes, and more recently in schools where I go on supply. It is in schools with a 'wider curriculum' and where children are allowed to develop and use their own methods, that they achieve at a far higher level in National Curriculum terms. Some possible reasons for this are given in Chapter 2, such as the need for number to have 'meaning' for children. So, if we are teaching for the highest attainment possible there are clear implications here for teaching styles.

4 It seems that children who are shown methods of how to do calculations, partially abandon their own methods (those established on the secure brick wall), but often do not fully understand the ones they are taught (part of the 'school maths' wall). In other words, when they have to calculate something in a school setting, they are often secure with *neither* method. This may be one explanation why so many errors appear in children's work when they try to write calculations down – an area in need of further research.

5 The child needs to have *his own mathematical thinking* opened up to him. The whole process must be related to some method that he already uses – to his secure 'brick wall', otherwise he is always operating on half power, on the second-hand methods of various teachers and maths schemes.

If we unlock children's own intuitive methods, (by emphasising and encouraging them), engage in specific teaching with apparatus that makes sense to them and relates to their intuitive methods, give them time to reflect, boost their self-esteem, make it a positive experience and a meaningful one, then they can operate at full power.

Doing this for a child is one of the most thrilling things in teaching! It's like that magic moment when a small child rushes up to you, her face glowing with pleasure and tells you that she can read. When those special moments come you can stand back and watch the child race off, powered with her own understanding. The success breeds more success and it is my experience that a child can go from being a poor performer to a child who can function well above the level that might be expected for her age.

That is the power of the child's intuitive methods.

Section B – Teacher's stories

This section comprises teachers' stories about their work with children. The stories are more or less arranged according to the age of the children.

$$213 - \\ 167$$

You cross out the 2 and put a 1, then you put a little 1 next to the 1, so that makes 11, then you cross out the 11 and put a 10, then you put a little 1 by the 3, and that makes 13 so you take 7 from the 13 .... er ... or is it 13 from 7.... er ... big from little ... er ... bottom from top ... so thats 7 from 13 is 6 so you put a 6 under the line and you carry a 10 ... no ... you borrow a 10 ... er ... no ... the 10 is on the top line, so, um ... maybe its not a take-away ... it might be an add ...

© *Joy Dunn*

—8— Nursery children explore maths
Sarah Killworth, Lesley Neilson and Sue Atkinson

Age	3–5
Situation	teachers with groups
Maths	the early language stage
Theme	classroom organisation; children's own methods and symbols; links with writing

Teachers working with children at the start of their formal education outside the home are aware of the need to provide plenty of varied experience at this crucial stage in the learning process. Children need to be involved in situations that make 'human sense' and to see meaning and purpose in their learning.

Language and activity hold the key

It cannot be emphasised enough that language development and children's activity at this stage are vital in their process of learning. The 'home' language of the children and their intuitive understandings are nurtured by sensitive adults, laying firm foundations for secure learning later on. It is also the stage when children seem to be given the most freedom in the education process – the freedom to play – to search actively for shared and personal meanings.

Of course, this is often what we might term 'structured play' because the equipment has been selected with particular learning experiences in mind. In this context the children explore, share, and use language to find their way towards the development of concepts, ideas and skills. They are constantly trying to give situations their own meaning.

Children explore

Hughes (1986) indicates that children at this stage are capable of a great deal. Sometimes adults do not see what meanings the children are giving to a situation, but by talking with them we can explore ideas together and try to see how the children are thinking. It is important to try to provide an exciting environment with plenty of opportunity to talk and explore.

Children experiment

Three children, Tracey, Jane and Gary, began with a book that showed children doing an investigation suspending magnets. The work was well under way before we noticed what the children were doing. At the start of the day we had put the magnets on the woodwork bench. We were using the bench as a conventional table, but wondered if the children perceived it as an area for construction which encouraged them in their task?

No adult was involved in the work except for discussion with the children about what they were doing, and listening to their language as they cut the string and threaded it through the chairs, working out how to suspend the magnets. One child, aged just four, 'read' the instructions to the other children from the magnet book. The activity lasted all morning and well into the afternoon. The children were willing to draw their work and write about it (Figure 8.1 on the next page) although this could not show the richness of the experience.

It is often not possible to divide up a young child's learning into the subjects of the National Curriculum but this one was very rich in mathematical language and covered a surprising number of the maths attainment targets – as well as attainment targets in English, science and technology. What was so exciting about talking to the children about what they had done, was that they had clearly been able to give the situation enormous meaning. Here was another brick placed firmly on the wall that has its foundations in early intuitive knowledge and experience.

Singing rhymes

Children as young as three join in enthusiastically with number songs like *Five little speckled frogs*. (See resource list at the back of the book for other number songs etc.) In our nursery we sing the song with five children pretending to be frogs, who, as we sing, jump into the pool one at a time. The other children hold up their five fingers, and it is clear that they are able to do the counting back one at a time accurately, matching the number of frogs to their number of fingers. We provide lots of other

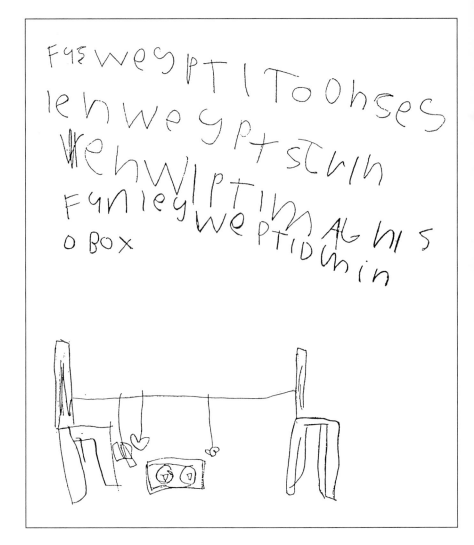

Figure 8.1 Jane
First we put two chairs together then we put some wool to each chair. And then we put a few pieces of wool hanging down and then we put some magnets on the pieces of wool hanging down. Finally we put two bits of magnets in a box.

situations for early counting experiences, like games, a shop, and of course the Play House. We aim to give the children confidence in their mathematical abilities and, where possible, involve the parents in our work.

A place to write and draw

In Lesley's nursery, they provided the children with a variety of writing tools, paper, and an old typewriter.

Melissa, a little girl aged four years and two months, who was working with the typewriter on which the '5' key was missing said, 'Look, I can count.' She began to type, counting as she went. 'Two, three, four . . . hmm . . .'(*knowing from experience that the 5 key was missing*) 'Let's pretend this is the five.' She pressed the 6 key but said, 'Five'. Then, pressing the 7 she said 'six', and so on, continuing counting in sequence.

The atmosphere at home and school is important in creating an environment in which children can use their own symbols and ideas

She seemed fully aware of what she was doing – using 'pretend' symbols, and when she had got to the end of the row of numbers on the typewriter and pressed the zero for 9, she hesitated and said, 'It's just pretend – that one is nine really,' pointing to the correct 9 key. Then, with a great flourish of satisfaction she said 'ten,' pressing two keys, the j and x; and 'eleven' pressing the k and x. At this point her counting broke down and she said 'fifteen, sixteen' but continued to choose letter keys to represent these numbers.

What is so interesting about this is the way that Melissa knew that she was not always using the conventional symbols for numbers, but was able to use others in their place. Her willingness to pretend and her lack of fear in telling an adult what she was doing is typical of young children's ability to use symbols to fit in with their own meaning.

Providing an accepting atmosphere at both home and school would seem to be very important in giving children the chance to explore early maths ideas in contexts which they can understand. (This point about children using their own symbols is explored further on p. 64 and 80 and by Marion Bird in her book *Mathematics For Young Children*.)

Mathematical writing

Sarah and Elizabeth, in their nursery, also give children a similar space to explore writing and the use of symbols in mathematical contexts. They have a huge table with pencils, crayons and felt tips in all shapes and sizes, along with plenty of paper. Children use the materials frequently. Arabell (aged four years and eight months) wrote down her recipe for hot cross buns. (Figure 8.2). When she read this back, she had included all the ingredients, and had remembered exactly what to do.

Figure 8.2 Arabell (4 yrs 8 mths)

Lubna (aged four) sat at the table making the staff coffee list. She asked for the teachers' names, 'small please', and then wrote the names down. She went to each teacher and asked them if they wanted coffee, ticking each name, and counting them up, before drawing three cups of coffee. She then put out three teachers' cups and helped to serve it.

There was no doubt about the meaning this had for Lubna and, as the weeks went by, she became increasingly confident in writing down mathematical ideas, usually using a mixture of her own symbols and conventional ones that she had remembered, or had asked an adult to draw for her to copy.

Figure 8.3 Samuel (4yrs 5mths)

Samuel (aged four years and five months) used numbers in a very interesting manner. It was not always easy to see what Samuel meant; indeed, we sometimes concluded that he may not have attached meaning to everything that he wrote. Figure 8.3 shows a typical example of his work. Samuel was unable to explain what he was doing, but this may have been a result of the fact that he lived in Uganda until he was three, and had problems communicating in English. What is important, however, is that we allowed him the chance to explore his own meaning. (It is also important to note that a few months later, in school, Samuel coped very well with mathematical tasks, showing a particular aptitude for maths. For example, on his second try, he managed to write the numbers on a circular clock face in the correct positions – a task that can often defeat an eight-year-old.)

Making maths explicit

Placing number apparatus on the writing table can prompt children to include maths in their writing. Shelly (aged four years and three months) wrote from the right saying 'One, two, three, four'. She used the conventional symbol for one at the start but, seeming unconcerned, 'pretended' the rest (see Figure 8.4). She was able to count the Unifix correctly up to seven, which indicated that her mathematical abilities clearly went beyond her abilities to use conventional symbols accurately.

Beth (aged four years and eight months) wrote 'five fishes' in a spontaneous response to a jigsaw (figure 8.5), and Lisa (aged three years and eleven months) tried to draw her brother's birthday cake with six candles (Figure 8.6).

It was very apparent that other children liked the opportunity to practice numbers in writing situations. Nadim (aged 4 years and nine months) showed that she liked to write numbers (Figure 8.7). She used

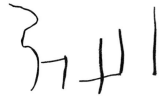

Figure 8.4 Shelly (4yrs 3mths)

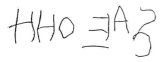

Figure 8.5 Beth (4yrs 8mths)

Figure 8.6 Lisa (3yrs 11mths)
A cake with 6 candles

Figure 8.7 Nadim (4 yrs 9 mths)

Figure 8.8 Samuel (4 yrs 5 mths)

all of these symbols conventionally and could count accurately up to eight. Samuel, mentioned earlier, showed a typical mixture of conventional, invented, and reversed symbols (Figure 8.8).

Figure 8.9 Clive (4 yrs 6 mths)
I will cut your hair this afternoon.
Come at 3 o'clock.

Figure 8.10 Gary (4 yrs 1 mth) A bill for £3

At the hairdressers

Creating a hairdressers as part of a topic about 'ourselves' led to some fascinating mathematical writing. Children were able to give their clients appointments in the large appointment book (Figure 8.9) and related appointment cards.

When the hair was washed, cut, curled and dried, clients were given a bill (Figure 8.10).

The baby shop

The children became very interested in photos of themselves as babies, so we decided to start a baby shop selling nappies, bottles, etc. Tania (aged four-and-a-half) stuck price labels on the goods (Figure 8.11), and the other children accepted her invented symbols and could remember the meanings.

Figure 8.11 Tania (4 yrs 6 mths)

2p

4p (written as To To)

5p (written as To To E)

— 9 — Young children's representations of number operations
Sue Gifford

Age	4 – 7
Situation	group with advisory teacher
Maths	calculator; number operations
Themes	children's own methods and use of invented symbols; links with writing

When do children start to use symbols to represent practical addition and subtraction situations? This was the question that arose from the work of Martin Hughes (1986b). He had found that not one of 90 'sum-fed' infants chose to use plus or minus signs to record practical addition and subtraction activities.

With the help of colleagues from the ILEA Abbey Wood Maths Centre, and from ILEA CAN project, I have collected various examples of children's own arithmetical recordings, including invented symbols. They point to the ingenuity of some children when faced with the problem of representing number operations.

Does the calculator help children to use standard symbols?

Being involved in working with six-year-olds and calculators (as part of the CAN project in ILEA), I wondered if the introduction of the calculator would help to make children more likely to use the standard symbols to record practical activities. I chose to do the 'yoghurt pots' activity with pairs of six-year-olds. Each pair had a pot with six nuts: one child had to turn over the pot, leaving some nuts out, and trapping a number under the pot for the other child to 'guess'. When they had become confident in doing this, I gave the children paper and pens and asked them, 'can you put something on paper to show all the different ways that you've found?' I assured them that they could show this in any way they liked. Initially they were unsure. Eventually they all set to work, except one child who did

63

nothing at all, insisting he could not think of any way of recording the activity.

The children had used a variety of ways of recording, including pictorial, written and symbolic, but none had used conventional symbols. I then realised that I was unclear how to assess or interpret the children's representations. Of the two children who chose a written mode of recording, Ashley (see Figure 9.1) produced a string of letters in a 'whole sentence' format, writing across the page, and apart from using numerals, using the conventions of written language. He read his work as, 'I can make two in and four out. I can make three in and three out.'

John, in contrast (see Figure 9.2) was more economical and read his work as, 'three in and three out, four in and two out, six in and none out, one in and five out.' This seemed to indicate a move towards abstraction in the elimination of superfluous words and so I judged this to be a more 'mathematical' piece of recording.

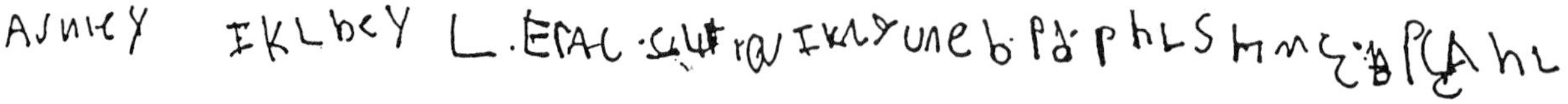

Figure 9.1 Ashley: I can make 2 in and 4 out. I can make 3 in and 3 out

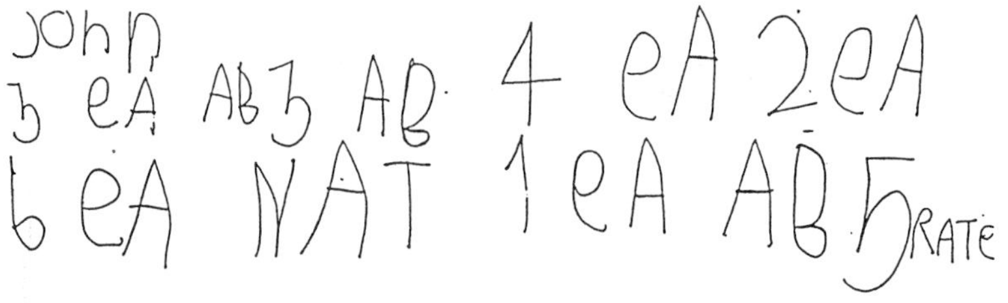

Figure 9.2 John: 3 in and 3 out, 4 in and 2 out,
6 in none out, 1 in and 5 out

Then I looked at Thu Hein's work (see Figure 9.3). She had chosen a pictorial mode for her recording. Far from abstracting key mathematical information, she had included minute details of the nuts, using the conventions of close observational drawing (encouraged by the school art policy at the time). I concluded that she may have been more interested in the nuts than my imposed request! I also realised that her perception of the task may have been quite different from mine: how was she to know why I wanted her to record? Not having any real purpose, how was she to decide that a simplified mathematical mode rather than an elaborate artistic one was called for? Perhaps she had done her best drawing to entertain me, or for me to put on the wall to show parents and visitors.

On the other hand, Thu Hein's work was arranged in a highly mathematical tabular form: there were, in effect, two columns of paired

Figure 9.3 Thu Hein

drawings showing the numbers of nuts in and out of the pot (and showing almost all the possible combinations, with no duplicates). I suddenly realised that, instead of a series of equations, such as 2 + 4 = 6, *which I had in mind*, she had used the most effective layout for recording number combinations. Hers was a pictorial version of a list of number pairs. In one way, then, Thu Hein's work was an effective mathematical representation, without being at all symbolic. (But then, by asking the children to record number *combinations*, I had presented no real need to represent *any operations*, symbolically or otherwise (something which I had overlooked). Was this evidence, in National Curriculum terms, of being able to 'record things systematically'? (See NAT 1 level 3)

Jancev was the other child who had used a pictorial mode to record, and she had used simplified drawings of the nuts, together with numbers (see Figure 9.4). This seemed more mathematical, as redundant details of

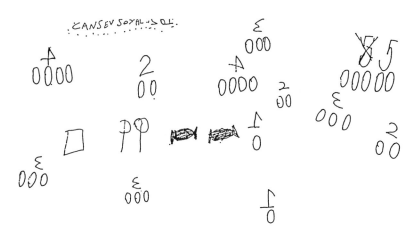

Figure 9.4 Jancev

nuts and pots had been omitted and helpful numbers added. Despite this apparent sophistication, Jancev's record is hard to comprehend. The pictures are dotted about all over the page. Although the pictures on the left, 4 and 2, or 3 and 3, may be intended as pairs, it is not possible to work out her intentions from the others. The need for pairing, or spatial organisation of some kind is evident.

Children do use symbols

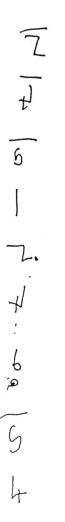

Figure 9.5 Katie: Plus 2, plus 4, plus 5 and 1, 2 and 4

One child did attempt to use symbols. Katie (see Figure 9.5) arranged numerals in a vertical column, alternating them with lines. She read her page as follows '*plus two, plus four, plus five and one, two and four*' . This seemed to show that the lines were intended as plus signs. What struck me about this was that although Katie does not know the plus sign and how to use it, she does know something about the conventions of written arithmetic, namely the vertical format. The fact is that you can combine numerals with signs which are called things like 'plus'. Exceptionally, what she did, unlike all the children in Hughes' sample, is recognise an arithmetical activity and attempt to use the appropriate written conventions. The reason for this possibly lay in my role as a maths consultant, known to the children as someone who regularly came to do maths with them. My presence no doubt signalled to Katie that this was a maths activity. Hughes' presence with the children he studied would not carry the same influence, and yet he had used obviously mathematical language like 'add' and 'take away' which could well have given some children a clue. Katie's readiness to use symbols is therefore not totally explained: perhaps her experience with the calculator (slight at this stage) or the novelty of writing arithmetic had produced positive attitudes?

Later I did the same activity with a group of six- and seven-year-olds, who were more arithmetically confident and so had ten counters in their yoghurt pots. To my surprise and delight, Susan *asked* if they could have paper to keep the scores, thereby supplying the children with their own purpose for recording. I subverted this by suggesting that they also make a note of the numbers of counters involved.

None of these children used whole sentences or pictures, and all used a vertical list format. Typically, Steven used numerals and the words, 'in' and 'out' for maximum brevity (see Figure 9.6). Sarah improved on this by grouping the 'ins' and 'outs' together, and so using a listed pairs format (see Figure 9.7). Then I spotted Susan, who was recording the activity by writing standard equations (see Figure 9.8). So much for total irrelevance of the operations symbols or of the equation format to this activity!

Interestingly, Susan had come from another school where she had done formal arithmetic. It seemed that she knew and understood the conventional way of recording number bonds, and had identified this as a 'number bonds' activity. Presumably, as with Katie, she had been able to

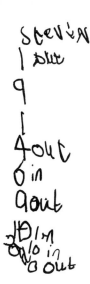

Figure 9.6 Steven

read the contextual clues (e.g. my presence) so as to select the appropriate format from her repertoire.

What happened next was intriguing: Sarah looked across at Susan's paper and copied Susan's last equation, 5 + 5 = 10. She then wrote at the top of her paper, 2 + 2 = 4. I presumed that she must have been thinking something like, 'Oh yes, it's one of those, like 2 + 2 = 4.' Perhaps she was attracted by the standard 'grown–up' style, or perhaps she liked copying Susan. Was this a link with her experience with the calculator, or another example of the fact that not all learning is acquired in school? Certainly Sarah was intrigued enough to make connections with her past experience.

In contrast to Hughes' findings, at least two or three children out of twelve were willing to use symbols to record a practical maths activity. It is hard to say why: the calculators may have had something to do with it, perhaps more through creating positive attitudes out of the novelty than through any great depth of understanding of the concepts.

Focusing on the operations

One question remained, When would the rest of the children use plus and minus signs to represent the actual operations of adding and subtracting? A practical 'function machine' box was suggested by a colleague, Val Heal (see Figure 9.9 on next page). The children have to guess the machine's function from the number of cubes going into and coming out of the box. The value of this activity lay in the focus on the operation being performed, the clear purpose for recording, a defined audience in

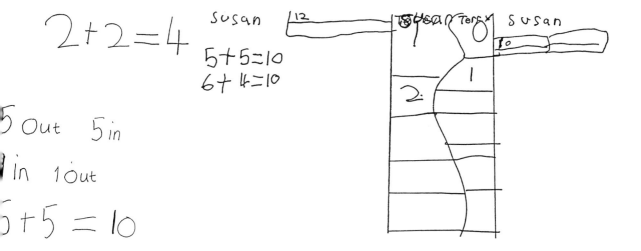

Figure 9.7 Sarah   Figure 9.8 Susan (The bit on the right is her way of keeping the score)

Figure 9.9 Function machine instructions

the writing of instructions for the machine operator, and a need for brevity forced by the size of the paper and the impatience of the children waiting to guess.

Initially, the children's instructions concerned the total number of cubes to be pushed out, rather than the number to be added or taken away. This difficulty in focusing on the operation rather than the total was what Hughes had also found. (I had assumed that a diet of sums had led to this, as sums usually require children to work out the total, rather than the operation. However these children were not used to sums, so I presume that operations are hard for six-year-olds to think about.)

The children then began to write statements like, 'three more' or 'put two', which they subsequently reduced to just '3m' and 'p2', thus using letters as symbols for the operations. Some children began using the equals sign, which they read as 'more' or 'plus'. (They had frequently referred to the equals key on the calculator as 'plus', perhaps because the equals key is frequently the one that produces the action, and so is more memorable.) Then one child altered the equals to plus, and after that plus and minus signs became common on the slips of paper. The signs were in various positions in relation to the numbers, to the left, right, or above.

Successive shorthanding

None of the children spontaneously saw the relevance of operations signs to this activity. With encouragement to think of 'quicker ways', however, they went through the process of 'successive shorthanding'. This is described by the Open University's course, 'Developing mathematical thinking' as the result of an approach which requires children to record activities in their own way, and by repetition of the same activity, to develop more economical forms in successive stages. Certainly the repetition of the activity gives the children time to see the redundancy of some information, to search for abbreviations, and to see the relevance of symbols, either their own, or standard forms.

Their use of symbols may have been related to experience with the calculator, or the similarity of the machine to it. As before, the children had no doubt that this was maths. Perhaps it was that in this activity, as Hughes puts it, 'symbolism serves a meaningful purpose'? Interestingly, they made no attempt to draw. Is this because, as Dufour-Janvier et. al. (1987), and others point out, language is better for capturing actions, while pictures are fine for amounts?

A meaningful context for symbols

It seems that children as young as five can find ways of representing operations. One interesting activity suggested by Hughes, which provides a meaningful context for symbols, is that of leaving a message to show how many counters have been secretly added to or removed from a box. If the others in the group know the original number in the box, the message helps them to work out how many there are in the box. Whereas Hughes suggested this as a way of introducing plus and minus symbols, Christine Pugh used it to suggest that children find their own ways of writing such messages. Jamie, aged five, devised a system for showing addition and subtraction, without the use of symbols (see Figure 9.10). He simply drew the pot, with the counters taken away shown at a distance, or the counters added shown in the pot. This record is very economical and within the familiar context, needs little or no explanation.

Another interesting example is that of Asif (see Figure 9.11), who did not so much invent symbols, as invent his own number sentence form. He was finding numbers that could be made with any combination of twos and fives, using colourfactor rods, and his teacher, Razia Begum, encouraged him to record his results in his own way with the purpose of discussing them with his teacher and classmates later. He simply wrote

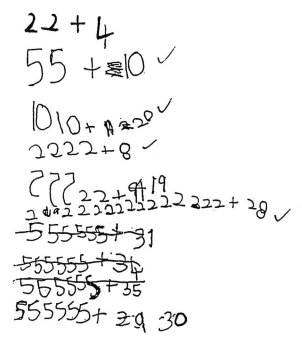

Figure 9.10 Jamie   Figure 9.11 Asif

down all the numbers used, then '+', then the total. He told me that he had written: 'Two, two, plus, four'. When I asked him what 'plus' meant, he explained, 'Two numbers put together,' (implying that the plus sign showed what you had to do with the whole list of numbers). He clearly understood his invented system, which was far more economical than the standard number sentence, and quite appropriate for the context. The one drawback of this system is that it does not distinguish between a single digit and a multiple digit number. However, the spacing indicates this and within the context, little confusion is likely to arise. This made me realise that a plus sign may be used by children as a separator rather than as an operator: that is, it performs a punctuation function rather than representing an abstract relationship.

Other children have tackled the problem of separating numbers in their own ways of recording and have got round it in a variety of ways. Sophie used a vertical list, under the heading of the total (see Figure 9.12). Another child wrote, 'two fours makes eight' leaving a gap between numbers as one does between words when writing and thereby making the multiplication sign redundant. Another child wrote, '11.2 is 22', which he read as, 'eleven twos is twenty-two'. Was the dot an invented symbol for multiplication, or merely keeping the numbers apart? This use of mathematical symbols to aid the layout of information underlines the lack of relevance of the operations signs to many contexts.

The invention of symbols

One situation which seems to give rise to the invention of symbols, is that of finding the difference between numbers. Perhaps this is because children are introduced to the minus sign as 'take away' and then have trouble relating it to 'how many more'? I have not found any infant age children who spontaneously represent such situations with a minus sign. I once asked two six-year-olds to show, in their own way, the game they were playing about finding the difference between two lots of counters, determined by a dice (see Figure 9.13). Tania's record is rich in mathematically superfluous detail, clearly showing her interpretation of my request as referring to the whole context. Melanie, however, homed in on the counters, indicating the difference by colouring in (as her Fletcher maths book did). When asked if she could show the difference in a quicker way, she put a line between the 7 and 8, which might be seen either as a separator, or as an invented symbol for difference, like a minus sign on its side. She read what she had done as 'the difference between 7 and 8 is 1'.

A similar symbol is used by Karen and read as 'You need four to get from 2 up to 6' (see Figure 9.14). Karen also circles the difference number: this common device clearly seems to serve a punctuating function, of emphasising the result of the calculation. Both these methods seem to fulfil admirably their purpose of providing an economical record, to be shared by people who already know the context well. Perhaps this shows one of the dangers of encouraging children to

Figure 9.12 Sophie

Melanie

Figure 9.13 Melanie and Tania

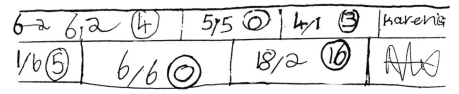

Figure 9.14 Karen

use standard symbols before they are ready. It may be that we too easily assume that children understand the concepts behind the symbols, whereas to children the signs are just a way of keeping numbers apart.

Other children invent forms which reflect the apparatus used in the activity. One example of this is Koysor (see Figure 9.15 overleaf), who was finding the difference between pairs of numbers on a number line. She used a 'skipping rope' type representation, which seems to reflect an idea of the distance between the numbers, especially as she then chose to indicate the pair with the greatest difference by the longest line. This method is highly effective for representing the idea of 'difference', and certainly seems more helpful for young children than a minus sign.

Another example was Peter, aged six. He was playing a game of 'higher and lower' with a dice numbered to 20 and a butter bean coloured blue on one side. With 20 as his starting number for the activity, he threw the dice and bean together: if he threw blue and 16 he guessed what 16 higher than 20 was. If the bean came up white, he guessed 16 lower than 20. He then checked his results on the calculator. To represent this he used an arrow either going up or down, (interestingly, rejecting the

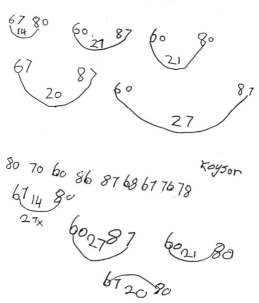

Figure 9.15 Koysor

calculator signs in favour of his own symbols). These seem to me a much more effective way of representing addition or subtraction, than the standard plus and minus symbols, which bear no relationship, visual or verbal, to the ideas that they represent, whereas the arrows reflect something of the essence of the operations. They may also reflect the language of the activity, and Peter's previous experience with a wooden number ladder.

You need to understand symbols to use a calculator

Children's difficulties with 'minus' in representing 'the difference' were underlined for me when I asked some children to select the appropriate keys on the calculator to check their results from the same practical game as Tania and Melanie played previously. Although they had been given more clues than children in the other activities, as far as having their options limited to the calculator keyboard, most children still had trouble, and started off adding the numbers. It was only by knowing the result that they were able to work out that it was the 'lowering key' they wanted, as one child put it. Those children who knew how to put two numbers into a calculator, and get a lower one on the display, could use the standard symbols to represent a practical problem. This seems to me one of the times when standard symbols are relevant and useful to young children: you need them to communicate with a calculator, if not with other people.

Eggs and chips

Finally, I would like to relate an example of a very young reception age child who demonstrated a readiness to use standard symbols in representing a practical problem. Some children were working with maths consultant Shirley Clarke on the 'school cook's problem'. This involved finding out what you could put on the children's plates if they were only allowed six things, and there were only eggs and chips. They had drawn pictures to represent the possibilities, added numbers to these, and then were asked if they wanted to write about what they had been doing. One child's writing, reproduced in Figure 9.16, seems to show an

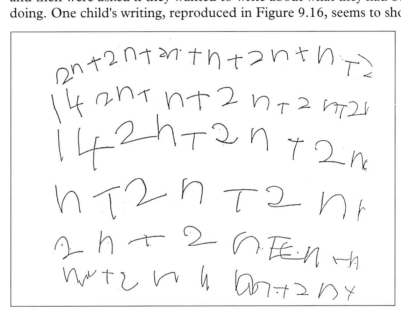

Figure 9.16 This was read by the child as 'There's 2 eggs and 4 chips and 3 eggs and 3 chips'

awareness that numerals and plus signs are appropriate in this context. This seems to indicate that some young children already know a lot about mathematical communication, the forms it takes, and the kinds of things it is used for, in much the same way as they know a lot about what writing looks like and what it is used for, before they understand it fully. And some children, given half a chance, demonstrate a readiness to try out their knowledge of mathematical conventions. Is this because they have not yet learned a fear of failure, or been shown the 'correct' way to do things?

How does maths relate to writing?

As regards this approach, I believe we can learn from current practice in teaching writing to young children, as proposed by the National Writing project (1989). This emphasises:

- writing for real purposes rather than just assessment;

- teachers responding to the content rather than the form in the first instance; and
- setting up a classroom ethos where children respond to each other's work, and discuss and compare different forms.

As with the English National Curriculum attainment targets we could put more emphasis in maths activities on selecting a style which is appropriate to the audience and purpose. It also means creating an atmosphere where, although standard forms are known from an early age, doing your own thing is doing it 'right'.

The implications of the national writing project for maths

So how does this approach fit in with mathematics teaching in the era of the National Curriculum? There are two main implications. Children using their own ways of recording maths are using notation systems that they understand and that are in their control. These systems give us valuable insights into the children's thinking and their understanding. On the other hand, children who are shown how to record may reveal only their compliance, rather than their understanding of operations and symbols. Secondly, we can use these insights to help children, and to move them on from non-standard forms whilst still maintaining understanding of what they are doing.

The non-statutory guidance emphasises the importance of children's own ways of working and recording:

'In developing skills in paper and pencil methods for calculations, pupils need to have opportunities to:

- record the results of operating with numbers in a variety of contexts and a variety of ways, e.g. recording work done with structural apparatus;

- develop informal, personal methods of recording calculations with pencil and paper;

- compare and discuss different pencil and paper approaches to calculations.' (E.34)

If children are encouraged to use their own methods, to choose from a range of forms and discuss these choices, they will be in a better position to select the right form for the context and audience, or, as the National Curriculum puts it, 'be able to record findings and present them in oral, written, or visual form as appropriate' (NAT 1 Level 4). Eventually this should make them better able at Level 10 'to use symbolisation with confidence'. Or was this what Asif and Peter, aged six, were doing?

This article first appeared in *Maths Teaching* (1990), the Journal of the Association of Teachers of Mathematics.

—10— Young children plan a picnic
Alison Base

Age	4 – 7
Situation	whole class with teacher
Maths	real problem solving
Themes	making maths meaningful; classroom organisation; teacher intervention

In this chapter, Alison, working on a course for her own professional development, had to plan some 'real problem solving'. It was rather daunting at first, but Alison's and the children's enjoyment shows up as she describes it.

I was teaching a small class in a two-class village school and had to decide on a project that would include some very basic maths, but would also provide some challenging problems for the seven-year-olds i.e. real problem solving.

Ideally, the real problem should have come from the children, but that isn't always easy – especially when you have a specific project to write up. I had some misgivings about making the decision of what we would do because the children might not have felt the problem real to them. However, I decided that a trip out for the day to a local beauty spot would appeal, and it seemed to have plenty of mathematical potential. I booked the minibus and cancelled our school meal. The children were rather anxious to hear there was no school dinner for that day, but they soon got excited about a picnic.

Though I had some ideas, I very much wanted to hand the problem over to the children. However, like most teachers, I can intervene far too much which takes the problem away from the children, but I think that you have to think out all the eventualities that might arise. It's not easy to sit back and let the children do it – especially when you first try it – as I was rapidly discovering.

First we had a brainstorming session (see Figure 10.1) with me as the scribe, writing down every idea to do with the problem. This is a way of getting the children to see the problem and to comprehend the many issues involved. As in all brainstorms, ideas flew around in all directions, with one little boy insisting that we take ice-cream! I could not just say, 'No, it will melt.'

The P.R.O.B.L.E.M.S acronym

Pose the problem – what is our problem? Can we do anything about it? (This works well as a brainstorming session where all ideas are valued and written down.)

Refining into areas for investigation – Decide what the problem is and what needs investigating (usually worked on by children dividing up into groups).

Outline the questions to ask – What do we need to find out? Will we be able to find the answers? Will the answers help us solve the problem?

Bring the data home – Collect the information needed.

Look for solutions – Can we find a clear result? Did the information answer our questions? What is the solution?

Establish recommendations – How can we fit the solution together? Who will be affected?

Make it happen – Get the solution into action. Does it work?

So what next?

Adapted from the Open University (1980) *Maths Across the Curriculum.* One of the structures for the course involves the process of solving problems, shown by the acronym. At any stage in this process it might be necessary to return to a previous stage.

Figure 10.1 The P.R.O.B.L.E.M.S acronym

Soon the children were all involved, and we sorted out the main questions, mostly about food.

- What sort of sandwich filling do we want?
- Shall we have brown bread or white?
- Shall we use butter or margarine?
- What shall we take to drink?

I divided the children up into small groups and we shared out the questions to be answered. They went off in their groups to sort out their own methods of collecting data through surveys and questions. It is important at this stage to let the children answer their questions in their own way because this is the only way that the problem will remain *their* problem.

I found it very interesting to see the different ways they tackled the questions. The children came up with far better ways of making surveys than my usual teacher approach. By allowing the children to do it their way, they learnt far more than if I had imposed a method on them. Sometimes their methods of gathering information didn't quite work out, like when one boy (aged five) copied out all the children's names on a piece of paper and went round asking whether children liked brown or white bread. He carefully ticked off each child as he asked them. When he reported back he realised that he had not actually recorded their answers!

Another boy, David, invented his own chart – a sandwich spider – writing down all the fillings his group could think of. Then each child had to tick those they liked and cross those they didn't – a very fair method. However, his 'sandwich spider' proved rather difficult to interpret; he had crosses and ticks all over the place, sometimes on top of each other. I let him go on with it for a bit because he is a very bright child, but he often has tremendous problems with presentation. In the end, when it came to analysing the results, the children could not count the ticks! The spider was a brilliant idea, but David hadn't quite carried it off. This led to some real learning for David about the importance of presentation – more meaningful than me nagging him.

Sometimes the children's methods of recording information were successful but unconventional. They attached enormous meaning to their own information gathering when it was their own way of doing it.

Once each small group had answered their questions and analysed their data, they came back to the whole class discussions and announced their results with great pride.

Some difficulties

Initially, the drinks group suffered from a common difficulty in real problem solving – dominant characters in the group making decisions on the basis of what *they* wanted. Two children carried out their drinks survey by 'looking' as if they were being fair. They wrote down a selection of drinks for their survey, but actually asked, 'You do like pineapple juice don't you?' They soon had to rethink as shouts of, 'That's not fair' went up from around the class. We talked as a group about how to make fair surveys.

Then they had another problem. Orange juice had proved the most popular, but I needed to examine the economics of providing orange juice for a whole class of children. The children in the drinks group came to see that they had still not asked themselves a basic question *How much drink do we need?'*

This sort of backtracking to basic questions happened again and again and is an important part of the learning process, especially when some answers to questions then generated new questions.

Making maths meaningful

When children are solving problems like this, they soon come to realise how mathematical ideas can help. They have a clear idea of what they are trying to do and so, when they use mathematical skills, it is in a meaningful context. For example, when the drinks group tried to solve the problem of how much drink they needed, we made a whole class decision to take two cupfuls each (more than this would mean too many loo visits!).

I intervened to tell the children that squash is sold in litres and the concentrate usually says how much squash it will make up with water. I also told them that the two adults going would be taking coffee so they were soon able to calculate that they needed thirty cupfuls of squash altogether.

Emma said to the others, 'Let's find how many cups make a litre.' Tasks were designated and the activity was done several times because they felt that 'Kate spilt too much!' They were very pleased with themselves when they were at last able to say 'Six cupfuls in the litre.' Kate and Anna then started on the next litre when Emma exclaimed, 'But we don't need to do it again!' The others looked perplexed and I had to be very encouraging to Emma at this point. I could see that she knew they did not need to repeat their investigation but she did not know how to explain it to the others.

Emma got thirty Unifix and put them into towers of six. I was not with them at this point but I could see that they were talking about it very excitedly. When they had made their discovery they rushed over to me and shouted 'We need five litres!'

The crisp group had found out the three favourite flavours by listing all the different flavours of crisps, and then doing a survey in which each child had to tick their three favourite flavours. Again, not how I would have approached it, but very fair. They could see that they would need to prevent arguments about who had which crisps at the picnic so they decided to mix them all up. Each of the three sorts came in six little bags and I had three bowls that we could take with us. The question was, how could they mix them up fairly so that no one had more of the Wotsits (the clear favourite)?

Once at the picnic I was impressed to see the very young children in this group share out the crisps into the three bowls. There was a great deal of discussion. Vicky could see she had six bags of each kind so she emptied one whole bag into one bowl, the next bag into the next bowl and the third bag into the third bowl. 'That's right,' she said, 'there's three left.' The others in her group could then see what she was doing and were quick to copy. So three five-year-olds solved their problem through division in a real and concrete way and got a great deal of satisfaction from it. Making something happen like this makes the maths very meaningful because the children know its purpose.

−11− Reception children write about their maths
Sue Atkinson

Age	5
Situation	group with class teacher
Maths	weighing
Themes	linking maths to writing; classroom organisation; children's own symbols

A reception class teacher describes how her class had a writing corner and were used to 'trying writing' in which they used their own symbols for their work. The teacher shows how she developed her own confidence in maths by using 'trying writing' to understand more of the children's mathematical thinking.

From the first day of term I found it fairly easy to get the children to write on their own, and to sit and 'read' with me. However, it was another thing to get them to think this way about maths. They were hung up on 'how do you write a five'. Of course, I had a number frieze and was actively teaching them their numbers, and intended to go on doing that, so I knew I had to relax about using a similar apprenticeship approach to maths, in the same way that I do for language.

In writing I go for confidence, for using the child's own intuitive methods, and I praise and encourage all along the line. I find it easy to make writing meaningful and of course the children enjoy it. The writing corner is well equipped and is always one of the most popular areas to work in.

I find that a great stimulus to getting children to write is to think of a very wide variety of writing situations, so cards, letters, lists, stories, rules for games, things to remember and captions for pictures are being written throughout the week. Many of these writing situations were more mathematical than I had at first realised, for example, rules for games or writing a sequence of events as when Stephen wanted to write down how to make a pop-up bird card. It seemed that if I wanted to have the same approach to maths as I do to language, I could help myself if I first concentrated on finding the maths within the work we were already doing.

The language stage

This process was much easier than I thought because as soon as I started listening to the children talking about their maths, I could see how much maths is dependent on language development. We talk of the early stages of maths learning as 'the language stage', and I realised that whatever maths they were doing (and it is important that they were actively doing something) the children found their way towards understanding it *through language.*

Integrating maths into other classroom activities

My task then, as the teacher, was to integrate maths much more into the ethos of the classroom, where children's own efforts to read and write are valued.

We set up a baker's shop and I suggested that the children should price label the things. Mary's price tags (see Figure 11.1) were accepted by the other children and I noticed that they could 'read' the prices for the whole six weeks that we had the shop. This acceptance of their own symbols for numbers seemed to be a turning point. It was clear that I had made far too clear a division between maths work and all the other work of the classroom, so I decided that it was far better for the children to do all their work in one book. This really paid off and from then on, I found that the children wrote more about their maths.

They would write about numbers, cooking, buying things at the baker's. I felt that not only was I becoming more accepting of maths being integrated into the rest of the classroom activity, but the children and parents were as well.

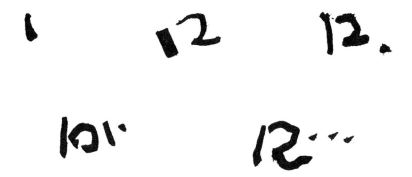

Figure 11.1 Mary's price tags for 1p   2p   3p   4p and 5p (5 yrs 1 mth)

Weighing the glo-bug

One day, Beccy was very interested in the bucket scales and she started trying to weigh her glo-bug – a toy she had brought to school. Weighing was an important feature of the shop and was a favourite activity, so I had put the scales on a table with some Unifix, conkers and bottle-tops. Beccy chose a group to work with her, and they set about weighing various objects.

I could not work with Beccy's group all the time as I was busy with reading, so after talking through with them what they had done, I suggested that they write about it so that they could read it to the others. These written records had many advantages.

1 The children enjoyed reading them to the class.

2 Several children made a display focusing on things they had weighed and made a book of their writing.

3 Writing integrated maths into the rest of the curriculum. I felt that these early maths experiences were meaningful – partly because I was giving the children *time to talk* as they wrote and drew.

4 The work was valuable for me to assess the level of individual children's understandings. For example, Katie's work (see Figure 11.2) shows no sign of any understanding that the scales balanced with the glo-bug in one side and twelve Unifix in the other. I thought when we were talking as a group that she had understood the idea of 'heavier than'. However, through her writing I could see that this was not the case. On checking this with her on her own, she was clearly vague about the whole concept of 'heavier', and what happens to the balance when you are comparing mass. The writing was giving me insight's into children's thinking that I might not otherwise have had.

Beccy's work (see Figure 11.3) showed a similar and common

Here is a glowbug
and unifix

Figure 11.2 Katie (5 yrs 1 mth) Here is a glo-bug and Unifix

Figure 11.3 Beccy (5 yrs 4 mths) The cubes are bigger than the glo-bug

misunderstanding, with 'biggest' being substituted for 'heaviest'. It was several weeks before she could grasp the idea of 'heavier' – yet in group discussion, I had missed this fact.

John and Barry, working together, showed the usual huge spread of ability I was dealing with. John merely drew the shoe, (see Figure 11.4) but Barry was totally confident about the whole task (see Figure 11.5).

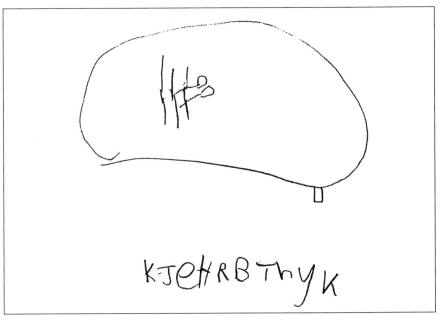

Figure 11.4 John (5 yrs 3 mths) Here is a black shoe

Figure 11.5 Barry (5yrs 2 mths) This is the scales with shoes in the scales.
Mine was heavier.

Reception class organisation

- Although I was using children's own symbols, I continued with all my usual teaching of standard symbols for numbers. This did not seem to cause any problems.

- The children used calculators and accepted their own notations alongside mine and the more angular ones of the calculator.

- Of course it is hard to measure one class against another, but I did think that this class was very alert to numbers and no one showed any sign of fear of maths.

- I used games to teach maths concepts and to teach the conventional signs for mathematical operations. (See Hughes, 1986b.)

- I felt more confident about teaching maths! I think that I am integrating it into the rest of the classroom experience.

- I started using a 'maths diary' in the children's book. I do not put an entry every day, but I get parents to help me if they have done an activity.

−12− A simple starting point
Marion Bird

Age	7 – 9
Situation	maths education lecturer with a group
Maths	a number investigation
Themes	children reflecting on their work; exploring ideas and generalising findings

Marion Bird writes about her work with a group where they explore maths from a simple starting point and look for ways of generalising their findings.

I asked the children to choose a number which was greater than 9 but less than 100. Wendy chose 52. I wrote '52' on a piece of paper in front of the group, then asked Debbie how many tens there were in it and Sally how many units there were left over. Both girls answered correctly. Then I asked the group which number we would obtain if we turned the digits '5' and '2' round the other way. Debbie said we would get 25. I asked Bora how many tens there were in 25 and Debbie how many units were left over. Both answered correctly. (I asked about the tens and units in both instances because I wanted to hint at the ideas that we could not just reverse the digits without making a big change to the actual numbers involved.)

I said that I would like each person in the group to work out what they would have left if they started with 52 and took 25 away from it. Debbie asked if they should write the sum on the pieces of paper I had given out before the start of the session, but I told the group that I did not mind how they worked out the subtraction. I waited until more than half the group were showing signs of having finished, then asked to hear the answers. Everyone who had finished had made the answer 27.

Jane had finished very early on and I took the opportunity of asking her how she had worked out the answer. She had not used paper but her description of what she had done revealed that she had managed to use the method of subtraction by decomposition in her head. She said, 'First I took 10 away from 50 and put it in the units. Then I took 5 away from that, that was 5, and added the 2, that made 7. Then I took 20 away.'

I also asked Debbie to tell us how she had worked hers out on paper. She said, 'I saw that there wasn't enough to take away 5 from the 2 so I exchanged one ten, put a circle round it . . . the 2 . . . and put a little 10 in it and then . . . I took . . . the 2 away from the 4 which was there and it added up to 27.' I realised that she had not really finished telling us about her calculation so I said, 'So the 2 from the 4 there (pointing) gives you 2 tens and the 5 from the . . .' (I hesitated here because I did not know if she had subtracted 5 from 10 or 12). She continued '. . .10 you've got 5 left and you add it on to 2 and it makes 5. . . 6 . . . 7, so it makes 7.' She also added that she was used to doing sums like that on worksheets and that she had got the idea of them!

I then invited each of the children to choose about five numbers between 9 and 100, to 'reverse' them, that was to turn them round the other way, and to take the smaller number from the larger number in each case. Again I stressed that I did not mind how the children worked out the subtractions, but I did suggest that they made a note of their pairs of numbers this time, in case we wanted to refer back to them.

Bora immediately recorded '99 − 99 = 0' and said he thought he had better not do any more of those! I think he felt I thought he was 'cheating'. I said that I thought he had come up with an interesting finding and wondered if he could suggest other numbers which would yield 0 too. His written record of his subsequent subtractions and comment is shown in Figure 12.1. Stacey also made the same observation and her written record of her thinking can be seen in Figure 12.2.

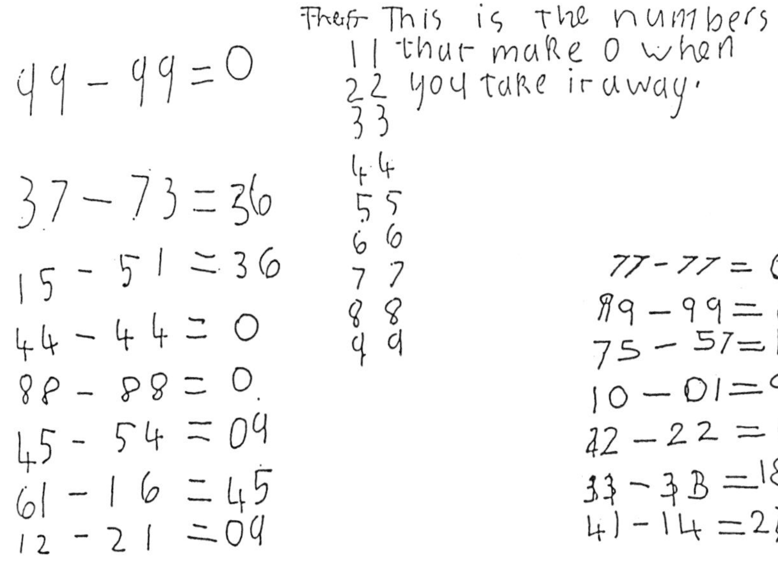

Figure 12.1 Bora

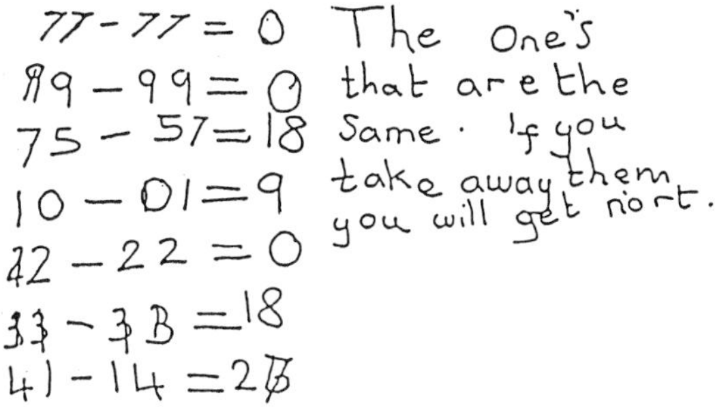

Figure 12.2 Stacey

Figure 12.3 Wendy

It is also evident from these two records that Stacey made sure she ended up with the larger number first in each of her other subtractions, whereas Bora did not. I made a mental note of talking with the children about the differences in how they were writing the numbers. Some of the other children did not just write the numbers down with the smaller ones first, they actually started to work out the subtractions like that. Wendy was a case in point as can be seen from the snippet of her work shown in Figure 12.3. She commented that she was stuck because she could not take 9 from 1 in the sum:

$$\begin{array}{r} 19 \\ -91 \\ \hline 8 \end{array}$$

I asked the rest of the group what they thought was wrong, to which Ray replied that she should have 'put the 91 down first'. It was interesting to note that Ray managed to decide which of the numbers in each of his pairs would come first before writing anything down: he did not have to make any alterations as can be seen from Figure 12.4.

I had plenty of opportunity to ask the children about other points in connection with their subtractions. As an example, I noticed that Linda had written the answer to 43 - 34 as 10 so I asked her how she had worked it out. She told me how she had exchanged a ten for ten units, then written ten little strokes for those, added 3 more strokes to them, crossed off 4 of them and then counted up how many were left. When she recounted she found that there were, in fact, 9 left, not 10. She corrected her record of her work, as can be seen in Figure 12.5.

Like Linda, several other children were tallying numbers either as stroked on paper, or with their fingers, then taking numbers off. Wendy suddenly announced, though, that she had found a quick way of 'taking away little numbers'. She said, 'Well, say if you had to take away 7 from

Figure 12.4 Ray

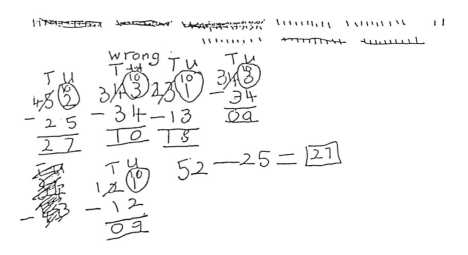

Figure 12.5 Linda

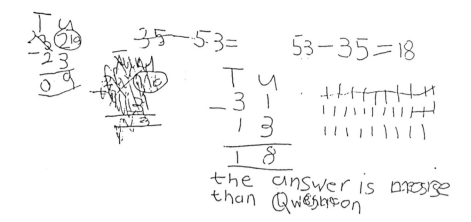

the answer is bigger than Qweshtion

Figure 12.6 Jane

12, well all you have to do is go 8, 9, 10, 11, 12 and that's the answer you get.' I asked her how this was different from 'taking numbers away' and she said she was 'adding on'. Bora said that was what he was doing too and it was a lot better than Linda's idea because it was taking her (Linda) some time to write down all the little lines! Linda subsequently tried the adding on idea.

Once the children had each carried out several subtractions, I asked them to stop, to look at their answers and to jot down anything they noticed. I did not expect them to recognise the answers as being numbers from the 9 times table because I knew that they had not considered that particular table in class, but I did wonder if anyone might notice about the digits adding to 9. This, however, was not the case.

Jane said that in one of her questions the answer was more than the question (see Figure 12.6). When I asked her what she meant she said that the 18 was more than the 'taking away bit'. Linda noticed that the first subtraction we had carried out was like that too.

Debbie said that for 75 - 57, 'I found that the amount that I took away was more than . . . less than . . . the answer I got left in the units.' She showed us how the 7 in the units of 57 was one less than the 8 in the units of the 18 (Figure 12.7). Wendy said that she had an example like that too and showed us her 51 - 15 = 36 example.

Amongst other things, Joyce noticed that two of her answers were the same (see Figure 12.8). This sparked off other children looking to see if some of their answers were the same too.

They are 1 more
Then you
took away

Figure 12.7 Debbie

two of my answres are both 18.

Figure 12.8 Joyce

87

72 − 27 = 45
91 − 19 = 72
81 − 18 = 63
51 − 15 = 36
52 − 45 = 9
94 − 49 = 45
61 − 16 = 45
73 − 37 = 36
75 − 57 = 18
97 − 79 = 18
31 − 83 = 18
86 − 68 = 18
21 − 12 = 9
10 − 1 = 9
76 − 67 = 9
32 − 23 = 9

88 − 88 = 0
22 − 22 = 0
77 − 77 =
41 − 14 = 27
63 − 36 = 27
30 − 3 27

Figure 12.9 Debbie

Indeed, in response to Joyce's remark, the children became very interested in comparing their answers, so I suggested we did just that. We collected together lots of different examples as can be seen in Debbie's record of the collection (Figure 12.9). The children were excited by the fact that they kept on finding examples with the same answers. I asked if they noticed anything about the numbers but they did not. I suggested that we wrote out the numbers in order to see if this showed anything more clearly. They called out the numbers in turn, starting from 0. Soon we had in front of us

0   9   18   27   36   45   63   72   (Note, no 54)

Suddenly, Stacey announced that the numbers went up in 9s! We counted on 9 from 9 to 18, then from 18 to 27, from 27 to 36, from 36 to 45 and 45 . . . some of the children called out 63 before others had finished counting, and were dismayed to find the rest came to 54! Much delight followed when Wendy then found that she had a subtraction on her paper which gave an answer of 54! (see Figure 12.10). Again there was excitement when counting on 9 from 54 gave us 63 and from 63 gave us 72.

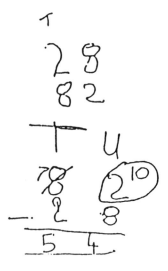

Figure 12.10 Wendy

Bora then said that we were not just adding on 9, we were sort of 'timesing by 9'. He had previously been doing work on counting sets of, say 3, with counting on in 3s. We went through the sequence of numbers to check that idea too and found that one lot of 9 gave us 9, two lots of 9 gave us 18, three lots of 9 gave us 27 and so on. Several then commented on the fact that we had found the 9 times table! Debbie also noticed how the units went down by one and the tens went up by one.

I asked the children if they had any ideas as to what we might try next. Joyce suggested picking pairs of answers and adding them up or subtracting them and seeing what we got for new answers. Stacey wanted to add up all the answers. Joyce suggested picking one number from each of the numbers in the original 'sums', but not in the answers, and adding them up. Bora suggested trying 3 digit numbers instead of 2 digit ones. The children chose one idea each and worked on it for the last quarter of an hour of the session. Examples of the written records of their ensuing work can be seen in Figures 12.11 to 12.14.

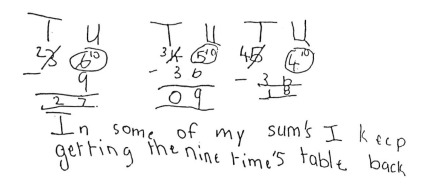

Figure 12.11 Wendy

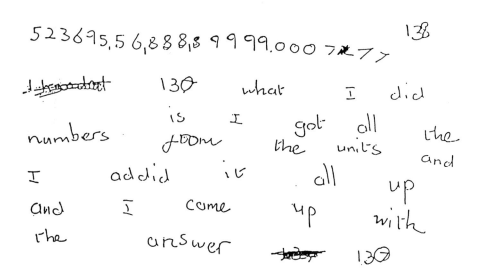

Figure 12.12 Linda

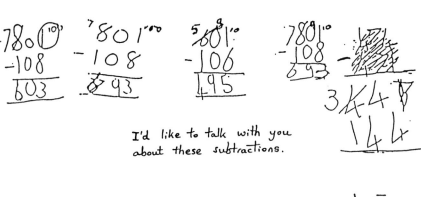

$$
\begin{array}{r}
7\,8\,0\,0 \\
-1\,0\,8 \\
\hline
6\,0\,3
\end{array}
\qquad
\begin{array}{r}
8\,0\,1 \\
-1\,0\,8 \\
\hline
8\,9\,3
\end{array}
\qquad
\begin{array}{r}
6\,0\,1 \\
-1\,0\,6 \\
\hline
4\,9\,5
\end{array}
\qquad
\begin{array}{r}
7\,8\,0\,1 \\
-1\,0\,8 \\
\hline
6\,9\,3
\end{array}
$$

$$
\begin{array}{r}
3\,4\,4\,8 \\
\hline
1\,4\,4
\end{array}
$$

I'd like to talk with you about these subtractions.

Figure 12.13 Joyce

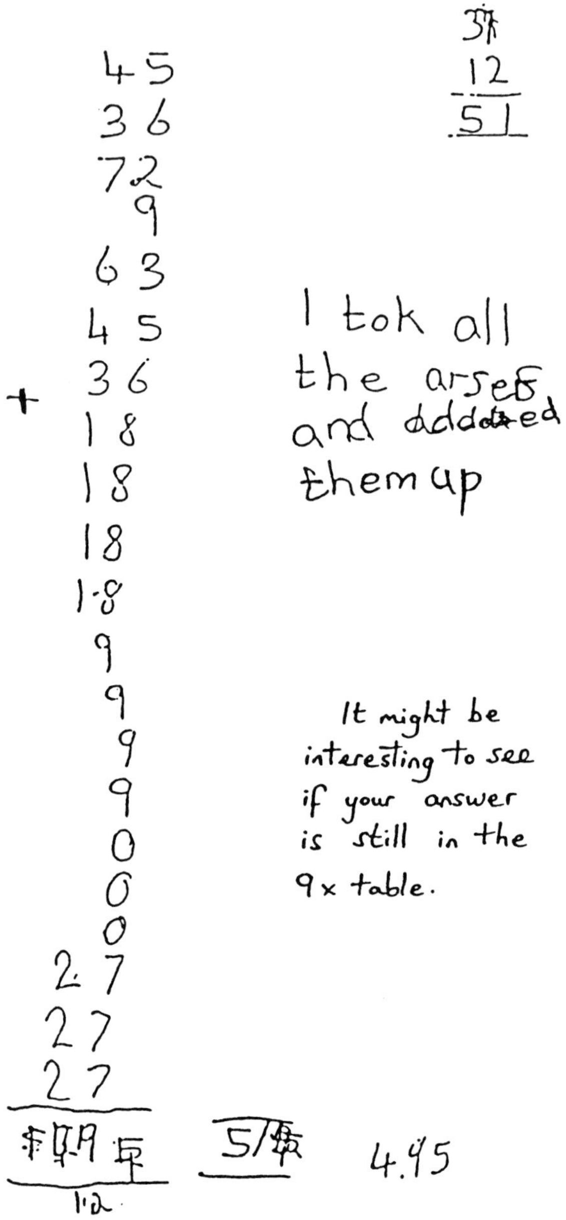

$$
\begin{array}{r}
4\,5 \\
3\,6 \\
7\,2 \\
9 \\
6\,3 \\
4\,5 \\
3\,6 \\
+\quad 1\,8 \\
1\,8 \\
1\,8 \\
1\cdot8 \\
9 \\
9 \\
9 \\
9 \\
0 \\
0 \\
0 \\
2\,7 \\
2\,7 \\
2\,7 \\
\hline
\end{array}
$$

$$
\begin{array}{r}
3\,1 \\
-\,1\,2 \\
\hline
.5\,1
\end{array}
$$

I tok all the arses and ddddeed them up

It might be interesting to see if your answer is still in the 9× table.

$$\boxed{1\cdot2}$$ $$5/6$$ $$4.95$$

Figure 12.14 Stacey

This extract has been reproduced from *Mathematics with seven and eight year olds*, with kind permission from the Mathematics Association

90

—13— Explode a number
Sue Atkinson and Alison Base

This chapter has been split into two parts – 'A' and 'B'. Part 'A' recounts work with seven- to nine-year olds and is written by Sue Atkinson; Part 'B' recounts work with five-year olds and is written by Alison Base.

A

Age	7–9
Situation	teacher with whole class in 30-minute lesson
Maths	investigating a number
Themes	children exploring their own ideas; teacher role

'Explode a number' is a name given to an activity in which the starting point is just a number and the children are free to explore and investigate it in any way they choose. The children were working on the number '18' at the end of a week in which all them had done an activity involving counting in 3s, building up to the 3 times table.

Children work on 18

I asked the children to investigate the number 18 in any way they wished. (I suggested that the children should start without using pencil and paper.) Here are some of the results.

1 Using the large place value boards and Dienes or Unifix.

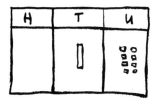

Figure 13.1 Using Dienes

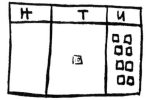

Figure 13.2 Using Unifix

2 Using Unifix place value boats. We talked about the similarities and differences with this one.

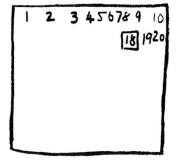

Figure 13.3 Using Unifix place value boats

Figure 13.4

3 With weights (I've given up trying to get children to call them masses!)

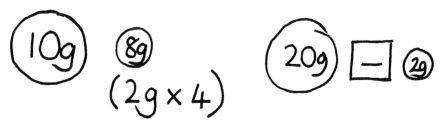

Figure 13.5

4 Unifix was used a great deal in various arrangements:

9 + 9, 14 + 4, (i.e. 14 red and 4 blue) 10 + 8 etc.

6 lots of 3, 1 set of 18, 2 lots of 9, 9 towers of 2 etc.

5 Using Unifix 'windows' on the 100 square.
– some put a 'window' every 18; some just marked where 18 was. Sarah had put a 'window' on every even number in yellow and on every third number in red and she said '18 is even and it's in the 3 times table. So is 12.' This led eventually to some work on prime numbers.

Some children had designed different layouts of the 100 squares (i.e. changing from the top row always being 1 to 10 with the bottom right-hand square being 100). This led to some interesting number patterns including spirals which the children explored later on triangular and hexagonal grid paper.

Figure 13.6

6 Using the Unifix number lines.
Some children just marked 18, but Jason marked 18, then counted on 18 and marked that. He went on with the sequence, on paper, up into the thousands, developing a confidence with large numbers that others began to share.

Figure 13.7

7 A great many children counted out 18 of something. (This does tend to be what children start with, but I intervene if children go on doing it.) Marie, a very low ability child, did a hoop like this:

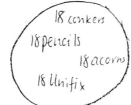

Figure 13.8

I was perplexed to know how to comment on this. I was so delighted that she had (mostly) got 18 of each item that in the end I decided that she should *check* her work but I wouldn't query her description of her work, 'I done a set of 18.' It seemed more important to boost her confidence and to let her feel success than to criticise her work.

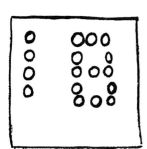

Figure 13.9

8 Pegs in pegboards are a great favourite to explore. This one used 18 pegs (see Figure 13.9).

9 Mark made an interesting one with straws. He said 'I made 9 crosses with 18 straws.' It was a moment to tell him about intersections.

Figure 13.10

10 Calculators are always used and many children bring in their own. It is difficult to see what is going on with calculators, especially when the game becomes 'Let's see who can do the biggest sum to get to 18.' The children became very confident with numbers because of their calculator work. Some could tell me they were doing 6 × 3=18 etc. and, as always, it is good to see that these children (who accept that using apparatus is a *good thing* not a babyish thing) will *check* what they are doing with Unifix, Dienes etc. I asked Ben to write down one of his 'big sums' (see Figure 13.11).

$$18 + 18 = 36 \times 9 = 324 \div 2 = 162 + 8 = 170$$
$$\div 5 = 34 \times 5 = 170$$
$$+ 10 + 18 = 198 - 190 + 10 = 18$$

Figure 13.11 Ben (7 yrs)

11 A ruler

Figure 13.12

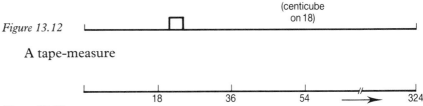
(centicube on 18)

A tape-measure

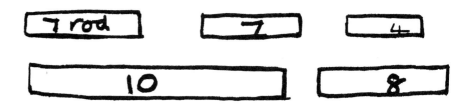

Figure 13.13

12 Interlocking cubes are always one of the most popular bits of apparatus. We constructed the 'Iron Man', made with 18 cubes (I had just finished reading the class the story).

'R' is the eighteenth letter of the alphabet and it was made with 18 cubes.

Figure 13.14 The Iron Man

Figure 13.15 The letter 'R'

Leon made a 'transformer' out of 18 cubes which changed from a robot to an 'attack plane'.

13 The school has hundreds of Cuisenaire rods and the children were very resourceful with them. Robert built an 18 cm high tower with them, and then another tower with 18 '10 rods'. Ryan counted out 18 'ten rods'. Shaun and he had a long discussion on whether it was 'right'. Shaun said, 'But 18 tens is 180.' Others tried variations on a theme of splitting up 18 (see Figure 13.16)

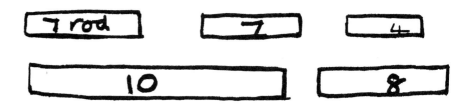

Figure 13.16

14 A bucket balance was used with 18 red Unifix balancing 18 blue Unifix. (I had been working on equations with them like this: 18 = 18

and had introduced the idea of the equals sign meaning each side 'balancing'.)

15 18 ml of water. Kelly said 'Three full medicine spoonfuls and a bit more.'

16 Barry, a nine-year-old with learning difficulties, needed a lot of help with the clock earlier in the term. He put the hands at 9:18 (almost) on his own.

17 Children used shapes a great deal. Carol (an eight-year-old with learning difficulties) made two hexagons out of the equilateral triangles then put the other six around the edge as shown in Figure 13.17. (I introduced an investigation using triangular gridsheets the next week to lead on from this.)

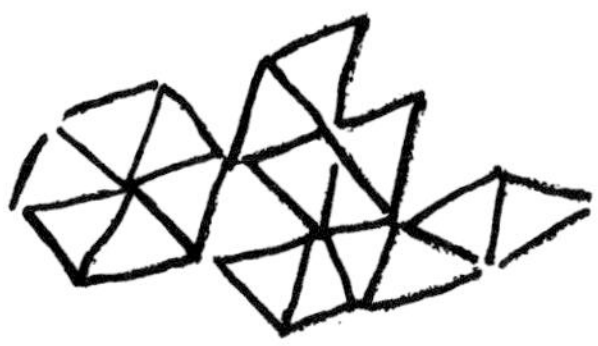

Figure 13.17

I could easily have over-intervened here to tell Carol she had enough triangles to make another hexagon. I asked her to tell me what she was doing. To my surprise she said '18 makes two groups of 6 and 6 left over.' We had just done a sharing activity when a child had brought in a bag of sweets for his birthday to share with the class. I had certainly not expected Carol of all people to say that.

Other uses of shape included numerous polydron ideas. Paul made a tower out of 18 polydrons that would support 500 g.

My role

My role as the children are working is very varied and has changed as the group have got used to investigating a number in this way. I noted the following things I did as the children worked.

1 I talked with parents and encouraged them to talk with children.

2 I talked with the children about what they were doing.

3 I listened to explanations from the children – this is a time when gaps in understanding show up.

4 I encouraged children to branch out, especially children who just counted out 18 things. I used open-ended suggestions like, 'Could you try to use a piece of apparatus that you have never worked with?' Or, for children who needed much more structure, 'You haven't done anything with a calculator/balance/Dienes blocks; could you try that now?'

5 I promoted the spread of ideas. This isn't copying, it is sharing and should be encouraged as generating the right sort of enquiring ethos in the classroom.

6 I injected language into situations where children's explanations needed extending, e.g. if they put out six groups of 3 Unifix and could *only* express it as '6 lots of 3', I would ask for ideas from others. If this failed to prompt discussion, I might suggest: '6 rows of 3', '6 towers of 3', '6 sets of 3'. I would then try to get the child to make a sentence out of the ideas.

Me: Let's see if you can put that all together in a sentence. Tell me about your Unifix group here.

Child: I've got 6 sets of 3 and it makes 18 altogether and I know it's 18 because I counted in 3s – 3, 6, 9, 12, 15, 18.

7 As I moved around the room I looked for opportunities to get children to generalise about what they were doing, e.g. '6 groups of 3 and 3 groups of 6 makes the same number.'

8 I noted down on my clipboard chart significant things for some individuals to put into their maths diary and notes for my own record keeping e.g.: *Sarah* saw 6×3 same as 3×6;
Sally used calculator confidently today.

Ending the session

I end sessions like this by giving the children two minutes to go around the class to look at the ideas of others. Then we all go around the classroom together and talk about some of the ideas. This getting together is a time for me to boost confidence, to praise and encourage. I regularly tell them what wonderful mathematicians they are.

I find this way of doing maths very exciting. Someone always comes up with something I would never think of, and everyone enjoys it. It keeps ideas ticking over and it is a good way of assessing children's difficulties and progress. This practical maths, where the children are free to create ideas for themselves, also presents a context that is *meaningful* for the children. It fulfils the conditions given by Martin Hughes, for the children to be able to integrate their accomplished informal ideas about maths with the language of 'school' maths.

B

Age	5
Situation	teacher with group
Maths	investigating the number 6
Themes	children exploring their own ideas

I first tried 'explode a number' when I was in my second year of teaching, sharing a class of 34 Year 1 and 2 children. I was really nervous about trying something different in maths, something not part of the scheme, but I thought I would give it a try.

This activity provides a good starting point for teachers exploring maths with reason. Working in this way we enable children to use and explore thier 'home' or intuitive maths, and we are creating situations in which children can explore their own methods of recording. The activity can be developed with older children too, e.g., 'How many ways can you arrange six squares (in a net) so that they make a cube?'

One afternoon, I found I was left with just ten five-year-olds, due to plenty of other helpers being to hand. I sat them on the carpet and began by reminding them of the other number work they had been doing recently. I then said, 'We're going to do some work about the number 6 today and I want you to use any of the apparatus on the carpet – shapes, beads, Unifix, pencil and paper – and see what you can show me about the number 6.'

Of course, I got lots of blank looks because it was something new. They didn't know what I meant, but they started very tentatively. I soon realised it was a mistake to have put out the paper, as one little girl went straight for it. The rest, of course, followed because it was a new situation. They all drew a number 6 and said, 'I've done it.' My heart sank, and I quickly got rid of the paper and said that we were going to 'explore the apparatus'.

Most of these children had only experienced maths as something that you do on pieces of paper so it was all very different for them. I therefore wasn't really too surprised that they were so stuck. I had to make lots of suggestions at first: 'You can make shapes with the bricks' or 'You could use the beads'. I tried to throw out ideas to reassure them and give them some ideas. Then a child made a picture of a man using six shapes. I called the others over to have a look at it, and from then on they were off.

The activity takes off

At first they just did the same – they all made a man with six shapes – but after about ten minutes I could have walked away and left them to it as they were so engrossed trying out different ideas. I stayed, though, because I wanted to observe them and to ask them questions.

They were very inventive and concentrated for the whole 50 minutes which was good considering how young they were and how hard I had been finding it to think of things that would keep them busy and interested for longer than a few minutes. I was also able to inject a lot of language and to ask probing questions.

Having done this activity, I now know to hide the pencil and paper and only bring it out when the children have explored the apparatus, so that they can record what they have done. This keeps the attention on the 'doing and talking', so they are thinking mathematically.

−14− Children working with numbers – discussion starters
Sue Atkinson

A Andrew

Age   4–7
Situation individual
Maths   addition
Theme   children's errors

'Andrew (aged six) was adding two numbers and repeatedly making the same mistake when using the number line provided on the workbook page (see Figure 14.1 below).

4 + 2 = 5   3 + 7 = 9   8 + 4 = 11

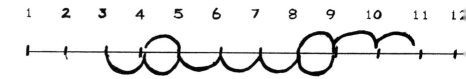

Figure 14.1

Questions for discussion

1 What do you think Andrew was doing?

2 How would you help him?

(Andrew was counting in the number he was on.)

B A bright group

Age	7–9
Situation	group with researcher
Maths	subtraction/place value
Theme	mental methods compared with written algorithms

A top maths group of eight- to nine-year-olds, described by their teacher as 'a bright lot', were asked to write down and work out, without looking at anyone else's work, '127 take away 84'.

18 children wrote: $127 - 84 = 43$ (correct answer)

1 child wrote: $127 - 84 = 53$

Out of the remaining children who chose to write it down vertically, as below, only 2 got it right – 15 got it wrong!

Errors in vertical forms included:

(1)	(2)	(3)	(4)
$\begin{array}{r} 127 \\ -\ 84 \\ \hline 143 \end{array}$	$\begin{array}{r} 127 \\ -\ 84 \\ \hline 163 \end{array}$	$\begin{array}{r} 127 \\ -84 \\ \hline 727 \end{array}$	$\begin{array}{r} \overset{1}{1}27 \\ 84 \\ \hline 88 \end{array}$

At story time at the end of the session, a similar problem was put to the children to work out *mentally*: $136 - 54$.

Although there are problems in assessing what individual children are actually thinking in a group session like this, it seemed that every child could work this out mentally. They had several different strategies, such as adding on, counting back, rounding up/down etc. Several used fingers and all seemed relaxed about their own method. The striking thing about this for the researcher was:

1 The enthusiasm with which the children described their own methods and the apparent ease with which they worked out this calculation with their own informal methods compared with the difficulties they seemed to encounter when writing it.

2 That even the children who got it wrong in the written form had no problem, it would seem, when it was worked out mentally.

3 The way their own teacher encouraged the children to 'do without apparatus now you are 8.'

Questions for discussion

1 Does this tell us something about writing problems vertically?

2 Did the children think that this was the *correct* way to write it?

C   Julie

Age   7–9
Situation individual
Maths   place value
Theme   children's errors

Julie's mother came to see me to tell me that Julie (aged eight) sometimes got upset in school because she kept getting her sums wrong. She wanted me to give Julie some extra lessons out of school. I had a chat with Julie who seemed an able child until we got onto the subject of maths, when she became cautious and defensive. I asked Julie what the problem was, and she said, 'I get lots of things wrong. I'm no good at adding.'

I got her to write down 26 add 32, then 327 add 143. She was able to do both of these calculations, but was quite unable to talk me through what she was doing, or why she was doing it.

```
(1)                    (2)
      26                    327
      32                    184
     ----                  ----
      58                    470
     ----                  ----
                             1
```

She had no explanation for why she put a 'little 1' under the line in the second sum. She just said 'That's how you do it.'

When asked to write down 43 add 8 she wrote this:

```
   43
   +8
   ----

  123
```

Me   Do you think you are right?
Julie   Don't know.
Me   How could you check?
Julie   Check?
Me   Yes. You know... 43 add 8 is 123... Are you right?
Julie   Don't know.
Me   Could you do it another way – 43 add 8?
Julie   (*Holding her head down and counting on her fingers*) It's 51.

A long conversation followed in which I tried to get Julie to decide which was right, 51 or 123. She was getting increasingly puzzled.

Julie   When you write it, it's 123, but when you do it on your fingers it's 51.
Me   So which is right?

Julie   123.

Me   Why?

Julie   Because you mustn't count on your fingers.

Questions for discussion

1 If you were Julie's mother what would you do?

2 If you were teaching Julie what would you do?

D   Ellie

Age	7–9
Situation	individual
Maths	subtraction
Theme	children's errors

Ellie (aged eight) was asked to write down a subtraction problem, 12 take away 4. She wrote: $12 \div 4 = 8$. She would regularly check with her teacher when faced with a new page of sums, and would say things like: 'Is it an add or a take away?' 'Will you show me how to do the first one?'

It was not surprising, therefore, that on most pages of her book the teacher had done two or three sums at the top first. Ellie would then do the rest, getting most of them right until the rule she was applying changed. So, for example, if part way down the page the sums changed from addition to subtraction, she would be unable to do this. She could follow a rule she was taught, but could not apply it in a new situation. She could not remember the different symbols for number operations like divide and multiply etc.

Questions for discussion

1 How would you help her?

2 What are the main problems that children face when they try to decode the use of conventional symbols?

3 Will calculators help children to understand the use of symbols more thoroughly?

E   Zoe uses symbols her own way

Age	7–11
Situation	individual in class
Maths	multiplication
Theme	children's own methods of recording and use of symbols

Zoe (aged eight) has her own way of multiplying large numbers. Figure 14.2 shows her method of splitting up the numbers, then multiplying them. She uses a conventional division sign in an unconventional way – for multiplying. Was she influenced by the use of table squares for multiplication?

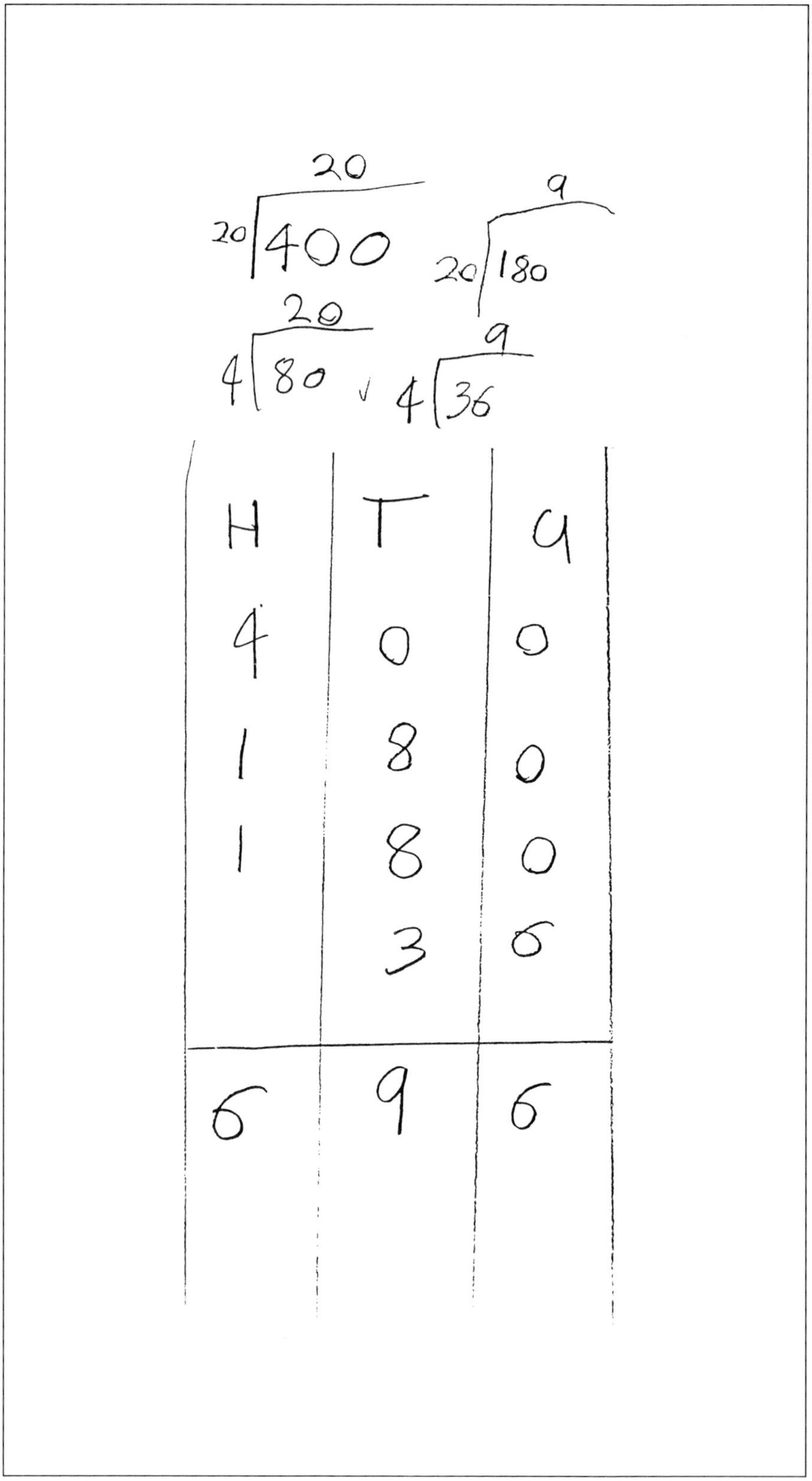

Figure 14.2 Zoe (8 yrs)

F William

Age   9–11
Situation   individual
Maths   place value
Theme   children's errors

William (aged ten) was very good at maths, but he was making a few errors in his work and it took his teacher some time to work out whether this was carelessness or due to some personal 'rule' that William was using.

(1)
```
 148
 234 +
 169
-----
 542
-----
 1 1
```

(2)
```
  48
   4 ×
-----
 183
   2
```

Questions for discussion

1 Can you see the 'rule' William was applying?

2 How would you help William if you were his teacher?

(William's rule was that in a 'carrying' situation he always put the smaller of the two numbers in the next column. So very often this would not show up, but in (1), where the units came to 21, he incorrectly put the smaller of the two numbers, the 1, in the tens column. When he multiplied 8 by 4 in (2) he got 32, and the 2 was put in the tens column.)

$-15-$ Tracey and Jason make a map
A maths advisory support teacher

Age	7–9
Situation	group
Maths	measurement and place value
Theme	children's errors; children's own methods of recording

I was suddenly accosted in the corridor by two children with a metre stick, a large piece of paper and a pencil each.

'What's after nine thousand, Miss, is it a million?'
'Well, not really,' I said.
'Told yer! Yer thick!'

I could see a fight brewing, so I hastily asked the children to explain to me what they were doing and I would see if I could help them. It was lunch time and the children knew this but said they wanted to finish their work. Their explanation of their task was that they were 'measuring the corridor'. I asked them to show me what they had done so far. (As this particular school seemed to have miles of corridor I wondered whether they had got the task right.)

Their drawings (see Figures 15.1, 15.2 and 15.3) were obviously clear to them, and as I was intrigued by them, I asked them to show me what they were doing. They showed me the way they had measured the corridor by putting down the metre rule, and I noted that they were not aware of the need to measure in a straight line, nor were they marking the point where the rule ended with any great accuracy. They used an adequate method, Tracey keeping her finger more or less still while she argued with Jason who was writing down the results. Tracey occasionally got up to hit Jason, then put her finger back somewhere near where it had been.

The crux of the problem as they saw it was that they had come to '9000' (Figure 15.1), so that next metre 'made it a million'. Or did it? Asking them about their recording in Figure 15.1, it seemed to me they were adding on 100 after each metre. 'It says 100 there, Miss,' pointing to the

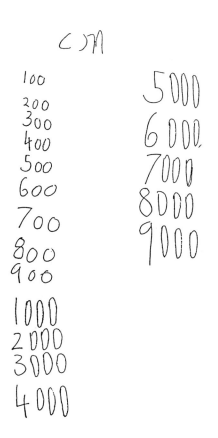

cm

100
200
300
400
500
600
700
800
900
1000
2000
3000
4000

5000
6000
7000
8000
9000

Figure 15.1 Tracy (8 yrs)
(Note this is cm for centimetres)

m

Figure 15.2 Jason
(Note this is m for metres)

20
30
40
50
60
70
90

Figure 15.3 Jason (9 yrs)

100 cm mark. (It transpired later in the conversation that they had not done this until they had changed who did the recording).

'So how long is this stick?' I asked, pointing to the metre rule.
'Hundred metres, Miss.'

So it seemed that they had recorded each metre as 100 metres, then at 900 metres, one more metre had been recorded as 1000, which seemed to show an inability to understand large numbers. Apart from their obvious errors of place value, they were clearly enjoying the work and it seemed to have great personal meaning for them.

'What are you going to do with your results?' I asked.
'We're going to make a map, ain't we Jason, an' we're going to get a "super-work" sticker.'

At this point a teacher appeared in the corridor and became very angry with the children. They were supposed to be outside. She took one look at their work and said, 'This is rubbish. It's not what I asked you to do at all.' Apparently they were supposed to be finding out how *wide* the corridor was.

Both the children looked upset and hurt so I cheerily told the teacher that I had been chatting to them and would try to 'sort them out'. I decided to get them to explain their recordings. Jason, who had been the first one to record the work (Figure 15.2), had 'tallied' up to 18 in a fascinating way. I asked him what he had done next. He pointed to a small corner of his paper (Figure 15.3) 'I done it quicker,' he said.

Figure 15.2, it seems, had been the start of their work, with Jason tallying each metre correctly, then realising that this was a slow method, he changed to the method shown in Figure 15.3, and tallied the odd one for 19, then wrote 20, then tallied 9 more before putting 30, and so on.

Tracey had then said that it was her turn to do the writing down, from a hundred metres, so she had done it on her paper (Figure 15.1). At this point they seemed to have stopped tallying and had recorded the next metre after 100 as '200' ('because it says 100 here, Miss,' pointing to the 100 cm). Tracey had recorded up in hundreds and they had now reached 9000, having gone from 900 to 1000, then to 2000 until they reached 9000. Their rationale for this was that they believed that 2000 was 100 more than 1000, and so on.

It was at this point that I met the children in the corridor and was faced with their question as to whether a million came next. I asked the children if I could photocopy their work, which they readily agreed to, and they were planning a way to get 'Miss' to let them finish after play.

At the end of the day I asked the teacher how they had got on. The teacher explained to me that both the children were 'stupid' and 'troublemakers' and that they were both unable to follow a task through, without fighting or causing chaos. I asked her what she thought of the work that they had done in the morning. 'Utter rubbish. I put it in the bin.'

Questions for discussion

1 What would you have done, or felt, as one of the children?

2 How would you react as a parent of one of the children?

3 What would you have done if you had been me? (A maths advisory support teacher.)

4 What would you have done as the teacher? (She was a supply teacher.)

−16− Children build a natural area and pond
Sue Atkinson

Age	7–9
Situation	whole class with teacher
Maths	real problem solving
Theme	the extensive range of maths; making maths meaningful

The school had undertaken a project to build a pond, and this was well under way when I talked with my class about what we might do for our problem solving activity. I was working on an Open University course at the time and, trying to be realistic, I decided to make the 'problem' the focus of the topic for the term. After taking a vote, 'making the natural area more interesting' came out as the favourite and the pond, although a separate project, became included in the work. I kept a diary of my observations throughout the term.

Brainstorming

We started with a brainstorming session, in which the children gave their ideas and these, in turn, were written down without evaluative comments. Much of my course was about encouraging teachers to stand back and let the children do the thinking, with the teacher as facilitator. Whilst agreeing with this philosophy, I could see that it was not going to be easy.

There we were in the first session, me armed with my large bit of paper and felt tip, and the children bubbling with ideas. Could I do this neutral writing up of everyone's ideas and keep myself from commenting? No, I could not. The children kept on asking me what I thought, and I was just too ready to tell them!

It was easily solved though. Wendy could write rapidly, so she and Amie became scribe and group leader, and I sat at the back and watched them in admiration as they threw out their ideas. They wanted to plant trees and bushes, grow flowers for butterflies, make homes for animals and generally improve the area to help in the conservation of the countryside, and also to provide a place for study.

Getting under way

Most of the things I had predicted did actually get suggested (so my own preliminary planning had been helpful) and the next day, with Wendy as scribe again, the children sorted out the ideas into a topic web (see Figure 16.1). The seven groups were plants, animals, soils, equipment, people, money, and rules. I intervened to get a balance within the groups, allowing friends to work together but also putting them in groups that would, I hoped, function well.

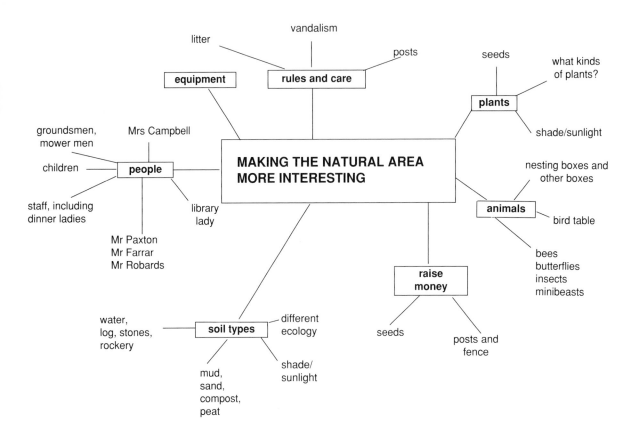

Figure 16.1 A topic web

By the end of the first week I was wishing that we had decided just to build a little garden instead of taking on an 80 metre strip of wild land! But the ecology books arrived from the library, gardening tools from homes, parents were offering help with plants and seeds, and there was no way I could stop the quite remarkable enthusiasm of the children.

The effects on the children

Some of the children were not too happy about the demands that the work made. Several needed a great deal of encouragement to work independently and to make their own decisions, then explain to the class group what they had done. I found story times and whole class times had to be more frequent than usual, and I had to do a lot of reassuring. On the other hand, Leigh and Jamie became incredibly bossy and tried to organise everybody's group. I realised that one sometimes has to discriminate positively in favour of girls in maths – or the boys might take over!

Going from whole class talking together, to small groups, then back to the whole class became the pattern for the work throughout the term. I thought that groups sharing their work in this way exposed the children to a very wide range of ideas.

How heavily should I intervene?

In trying to take more of a back seat I was watching my interventions very carefully, and realised that sometimes it is necessary to make heavy interventions. I had a problem getting the children to see that unless they actually did something quickly, they would never be able to implement one of their main ideas, which was to keep all the other children out of the area (it bordered the playground). They also needed to show the mower men the area which we wanted left to go wild. (The children had telephoned them.) Daniel had explained in a school assembly what the class's intentions were, but although the other children thought it a brilliant idea, it was hard for them to remember that this area was not for playing in. Christopher wanted a six foot wire fence around it, and I had quite a problem in scaling this down to something we could afford. I was perhaps more motivated to do this than the children were, having caught the mower man in mid-cut one day after school. My first wrangle with this tenacious and formidable man made me realise that speed and the odd heavy intervention might be called for to prevent the children's intense frustration.

A play-time raid into the depths of the games cupboard revealed a few assorted cricket stumps, so armed with these and a ball of string, a 'fence' was started. The effect was immediate. The five-year-olds stood in admiration as my class, rather bossily I thought, hammered in stumps, tied on string and announced that from now on, no one was to go in to the area without permission!

The 'rules' group came to realise the importance of politeness, and after a questionnaire was sent to each class, a very sensible list of rules was drawn up. My colleagues were incredibly understanding about the paramilitary way that this group patrolled the area and they brought their children out to the natural area for my class to explain what they were doing. This was very successful and I noticed how my class were functioning well as a whole group. They had a great sense of purpose, and those children whom I had worried about working out of my sight, were so absorbed in it all that, although fights did break out, they seemed to be about things like how big they could make the boggy area, so at least they were 'on task'!

Lack of money

The children decided that one of their biggest problems was lack of money to buy things like a buddleia to attract butterflies. They decided to hold a play-time sale of second-hand comics and toys. This was a major problem-solving event in itself and was very successful. The children then telephoned a local garden centre to see if they had a buddleia and one lunch time we went off to buy it. The staff at the garden centre seemed to find it amusing – me taking photos, the bags of coins to pay for it – and Christopher wanting to buy a gnome!

Once we returned with the buddleia (but not the gnome) things really started to happen. Parents said that they had never seen their children so excited about something at school, and I had never experienced such splendid parental support. One family brought in an enormous log from their garden, balancing it on a wheelbarrow.

The big log

The 'big log' became the favourite place for a group to retire to in order to 'sort something out', and it also provided us with shade. There were no large trees in the school grounds, so now with some shade available the children persuaded someone's grannie to part with some of her bluebells. But where should we put them in relation to the log so that they would be in shade? This led to some marvellous investigations and one group became so fascinated that they made a book about shadows, sun-dials and ways of measuring time.

I was astonished at the level of ecological understanding exhibited by the children. This was partly because of the good library books, but also because of very helpful parental input. One of the chief aims for the children seemed to be to get many different soil types represented. The children made good suggestions such as, 'If we have lots of different kinds of soil, then we will be able to have more kinds of plants.'

Someone gave us a huge piece of black plastic and the 'boggy area' was born. The soil mound left over from digging the pond was already colonised by certain plants so the fact that some plants liked specific conditions was easy to see. Someone donated two used 'gro-bags' of peat. A book about limestone plants led to the idea of trying to grow lime-loving plants.

The 'animals groups' planned a stony area for minibeasts, a bird bath, and a bird table (which Scott and his dad made one weekend). They also wanted to make a little house for animals in the snow.

The pond

My favourite time came when we began to concrete the base of the pond. 'The men' (some of the teachers' husbands) had decided that we needed 'two yards' of sand to do the job. This meant two 'cubic yards' and this was the signal for me to do some specific teaching on what a cubic yard was. We borrowed every metre rule we could find and a few rounders posts, and strung together two cubic yards. The children looked at them, and then they looked at the hole dug for the pond, a rather modest affair, and Alison, just seven-years-old said, '*Two* cubic yards seems an awful lot of sand.'

'Well, perhaps the men are wrong,' I said, 'I think they only estimated it.' There was a terrible silence at the thought that teachers' husbands could be wrong. Alison, a liberated child, was very quiet for awhile, then announced that her group would like to work out how much sand we really needed.

A question to one of 'the men' revealed that the concrete was to be four to five inches thick. It was no problem to find out how big the pond was, as groups had been drawing scale maps of it for the master plan of the whole area, but of course, these measurements did not give them the surface area of the bottom of the hole. It took a few days for them to solve that one.

All their efforts to try to represent the slope on squared paper failed. They were quite clear about their problem. 'When you draw a map of it, it will always be smaller,' said Amie. They then tried what I thought was a really remarkable idea. They made a cuboid out of centicubes about four to five inches thick, (all the transferring from metric to imperial measurements clearly worried me far more than it did them.) They explained to the rest of the class that this was as thick as the concrete and they were going to see how many times it would fit into the surface of the dug out pond. Listening to them explain why a scale drawing could not give them the information they needed because of the slope was almost the highlight of my teaching career.

They could see that their biggest problem would be the time that the measuring with their cuboid would take and how would they be able to mark the soil to show which bits they had already measured, 'String?' suggested Daniel.

So the next day they made a start on counting how many of their cuboids fitted onto the soil surface, marking where they were up to with string, but it was slow progress. When I was next aware of them they had moved from the pond and were working in the paved courtyard next to the classroom. When they explained their work I was forever converted to real problem solving as a way of teaching maths.

In the process of using the string to plot out the bits of the pond that they had already measured, they had realised that laying the string across the base of the pond would mean they could then stretch out the string into the size of the surface area. So they cut several lengths as informal measures and had taken these lengths of string into the courtyard, laid them down and drawn a large chalk oval that represented the surface area of the bottom of the pond. 'Our oval is bigger though because of the corners, so we will have to take a bit away,' said Amie. 'It's like when we did 3-D shapes at Christmas, you can't get the round bits, they get all scrunched up.'

They had remembered their abortive attempt to make a sphere six months previously and had been able to translate that experience into this work. They were quite confident that their method would work and I thought that despite its complexity, many of the other children were also following the thinking. This seemed to me to be the best maths I had ever done with children, but more was to come.

Using the courtyard

The group of girls waited behind as the other children left the room and begged to be allowed to stay in at lunch time. They wanted to change the size of their cuboid, 'because of the squares in the courtyard'. They wanted to make their cuboid into a cube that would fit a regular number of times into the paving stones in the courtyard. This involved an intriguing bit of division work, but when afternoon school started they were ready to get on with counting how many of their cubes would cover the pond base.

They needed 25 of their cubes for one paving stone, 'So we don't need to count all those middle ones,' said Wendy. They realised that they did not need to count all the whole paving stones in their oval, because each one would measure 25. They only needed to count up how many cubes fitted into the little odd bits at the edges of their chalked oval (see Figure 16.2), minus an estimate of 'the scrunched up bits'.

To cut a long story short, they worked out that one cubic yard of sand would be more than enough. They were a bit put out that two cubic yards were ordered! The smiles on their faces at the huge pile of left over sand after an evening of concreting was wonderful! Before nine o'clock in the morning they had got permission for the sand to be used to make a sandy area, and the theme of that day became how big the sandy area should be.

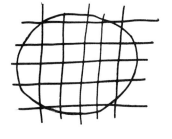

Figure 16.2

Money, again

Lack of money remained a perpetual problem – a good life skill to be learning – so for the summer fête the children decided to run their own games and use the money that they raised. Devising suitable games involved more maths in one week that I used to do in one term!

The most popular game involved throwing balls into a bucket propped up at just the right angle to make it difficult for the ball to stay in. If the ball did stay in, the prize was ten pence. Getting this game organised had involved hours of research into the most bouncy ball, the best distance

TB. 3.9   ~~SM 3p B~~
~~AFB~~   BRB. 53.6

dropped from 1 metre

tennis	60cm	53cm	~~50cm~~	60cm	57cm	53cm	55cm	51cm	52cm	51cm	51cm
airflow	~~38cm~~ 40	35cm		47	40	34	33	31	35	40	40	40
~~lg sponge~~	40cm										
5m sponge	~~45cm~~	53	46	39	43	40	43	43	34	43	50	51
blue rubber	50cm	52	55	50	57	58	57	54	45	55	53

~~3°~~ bounces out
30° bounces to 35cm   2m 90cm

40° bounced out
35° bounced out
50° bounced out

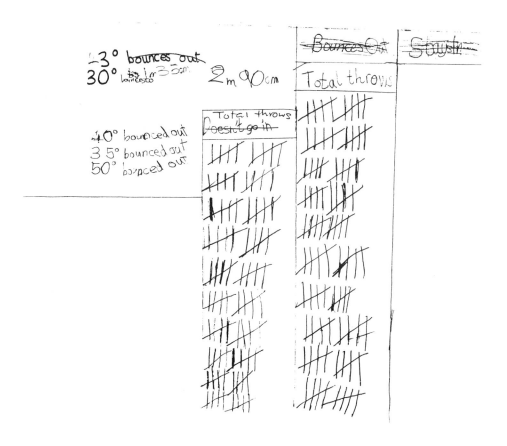

Figure 16.3 Children's recording of tests

113

for throwers, the best angle to prop up the bucket, and the probability of balls coming out. Similar maths was involved in the other games and the children recorded their results in their own way (see Figure 16.3 on previous page).

Scale maps

The scale maps the children worked on to plan out the different features of the natural area were criticised by other groups because they were 'too small to show the fence', so they had to re-draw them. The group that worked on the maps seemed to me to be using mathematical skills at a far higher level than I had been expecting. This seemed to be true for the whole term, for most of the children.

The following list shows the range of maths that one group encountered throughout the project.

Estimating the total money that could be raised.
Costing for each game in the fête – worked out from the probability of people winning.
Counting money, giving change.
Designing a rota of children available at certain times during the fête.
Finding the best angle for the bucket.
Making a rating scale of the best bucket angle.
Making a rating scale of the bounciest ball.
Measuring the height for the bounce of balls.
Finding averages of results.
Using a calculator.
Dealing with decimals.
Using a spirit level, clinometer, protractor, plumb-line.
Designing a 'fair' test.
Recording results on a table.
Working out percentages – for VAT purposes.
Comparing prices before buying.
Comparing discounts in percent.
Working out map directions and compass bearings.
Estimating the time in journeys.
Investigating shadows – movement of the sun – time.
Drawing up a balance sheet of expenditure.

This group also took on the organisation of the Grand Opening which included:

Planning the areas where classes were to stand.
Organising a length of ribbon for the ceremony.
Working out a timetable of events.
Calculating the mileage for the guest of honour's petrol money.
Calculating the cost of petrol per mile.

Other groups had similar wide experiences of maths, and in National Curriculum terms, these spanned most of the attainment targets, except algebra.

I had no idea that this work would have covered this range, or this depth of maths. It was obvious to me and the parents that the children were coping well with things like angles, averages and decimal points on the calculator. When the children needed to be taught a particular skill or concept, I did a straightforward exposition rooting what I taught within the 'real' problem that had arisen. Of course, there was a great deal of maths that they were only getting a glimpse of, and I would need to return to it at a later date to cover it in more detail. However, I was getting a clear picture of what each child understood, because they were having to think mathematically, and were not just manipulating numbers in a text book.

A profile of a slow learner

For my course, I had to write a profile of a 'slow' child, and Carol was my obvious choice. She had a 'thing' about maths – a maths block and was unable to count out reliably ten Unifix. She had severe orientation problems that showed up in 'mirror writing' and number reversals, and clearly somewhere along the line she had got lost in maths.

One of the biggest surprises of the natural area project was the amount of maths that Carol *could* cope with. In her 'diet' of maths for the term, Carol coped with large numbers (above 100), angles on a clinometer, division on a calculator, and adding up the 13 pounds from the playground sale. She could not manage any of this on her own – her problems were very deep – but I felt rather ashamed of the way that I had, up until then, confined her to such simple work.

Observing Carol carefully throughout the term, I detected considerable disinterest in the project at times. I decided that this was not so much that she found the project boring, or difficult, but that she was being successful and enjoying maths! Her disinterest was, I think, her way of retreating into 'I'm hopeless at maths and that is safe because you can expect nothing of me' which gave us a useful insight into her problems.

A profile of a bright child

Jamie would cope with most things. He was a confident and very able child. He could work out quite complex things, such as petrol money for visits to the garden centre etc., provided he had plenty of time. However, he sometimes surprised me. For example, he got incredibly bogged down adding up the fête money. I thought Jamie's recent experience in a very formal school became obvious, and at times he was at a disadvantage because of this. For example, he could do division on paper far better than the others, but in the 'real' situations that were arising, they could 'share' but Jamie was left confused, asking me 'what kind of sum is it?' This was a considerable shock to me. I regarded Jamie as one of the brightest children I had ever taught. That he was unable, many times, to see how to *apply* his knowledge was fascinating. It was so good to see his face light up on realising the significance of various things he 'knew' and it helped me to see that basing maths teaching on 'real' situations was a good way forward.

Conclusion

Writing this conclusion some years after doing the work, I know that I still feel, to some extent, insecure teaching maths in this way. However, I will not turn back from it, it has proved too beneficial for children and there are too many big issues at stake. The insecurity is partly due to the fact that it challenges me as a teacher. It isn't 'safe' to teach this way because it frequently surprises me and challenges my assumptions. It raises questions which I know I must try to answer if I am to go on growing professionally.

I recognised while doing this work what I intuitively believed, that this way of teaching gets the very best from children. Whenever I do this kind of problem solving, I get exactly the same reaction – enormous enthusiasm from children and parents and remarkable levels of achievement in maths from the children.

As my educational philosophy is founded on my respect for the child, to approach maths – and all the other areas of the curriculum – in this way, it is consistent with my belief. When the child learns, I learn too. It is by observing the child, by listening to her, by saying, 'What do you think, Amie?', that I am able to be co-learner, partner and explorer of our exciting world.

Implicit in this, is the much talked of belief that the child needs to be 'active' in her own learning. A great deal said about this in terms of 'child-centred' education seems to miss out the real corner-stone of this 'activity' – this co-learning and the importance of the relationship between the teacher and child. It is in my relationship with a child that I express my respect, my openness and my wish to try to stand in her shoes. By doing this I can draw out of her the intuitive 'home' learning that is shaping how she sees the world. This can then be built on, and her learning is secure and able to be applied in other situations.

This way of teaching is distinctively different from what many people seem to mean by 'child-centred'. I have an agenda, and make it quite explicit to the children. There is a curriculum to cover and a long-term aim in mind – the child as a confident mathematician and solver of problems. Sometimes I have to be very demanding of the children. Sometimes I have to intervene very heavily. I often have to give the children the language they need in order to express things in a mathematically accurate way.

It seems to me that this is the role that I play in the classroom in every area of the curriculum – it is not distinctive to maths. It is, I believe, a role that is part of true education – a drawing out. Not just drawing out of the child what she can do, but drawing out from the teacher too, within relationships in which, to some extent, all parties feel vulnerable. But that is the strength of working in this way. It is 'open' and 'real' in the sense that it mirrors good relationships within the 'real' world beyond school. That is why, demanding though it is, I choose to teach in this way.

—17— A young teacher starts off with maths with reason
Jenny, a primary teacher

Age	9–11
Situation	young teacher with whole class
Maths	fractions, division, 'activity' maths
Theme	text books leave huge gaps

Jenny works in a Primary School where all the teachers use the maths scheme in such a way that the children work on it individually. From the age of about eight, the children are encouraged to work without apparatus. What follows, is Jenny's own account.

I teach nine and ten-year-olds who come from a class where maths is taught entirely from a text book and examples on the board. This is nearly all what I call 'traditional' arithmetic, and my colleague in this class insists that by the age of eight the children should be working without any apparatus. We have lots of good discussions about our different approaches!

My colleague certainly can get children who are bright up to what she calls 'a good standard', and of course the parents really appreciate this.

Is is just a case of getting a 'good standard'?

I think that the 'good standard' hides some anomalies. Of course I want the children's work to be of a high standard too, but each year I find that the children I get from this class do not understand much of what they have been 'taught'. So each September, my intake – 34 children this year – is something of a challenge. There is, of course, a 'Cockroft seven-year difference' i.e. some children function like six-year-olds and some like thirteen-year-olds. I find that many of the children dislike maths and are extremely competitive about it. There is constant comment about who is on which book from both children and parents, and lots of parents buy their children the next book in the scheme to try to push them on.

I'm not against 'pushing' children. I expect the bright ones to do extra demanding tasks and I'm not at all against parents helping. I like to involve parents as much as possible. The trouble is that I find that children have 'done the book' but don't understand what they have done when asked to apply it, or even to explain what they have done.

Children do not sufficiently understand book-taught maths

The sort of thing that makes me feel that my thinking is on the right lines is an incident that happened the other day. Karen showed me that she could do long division. She could too! I gave her one to do and she got it right. She couldn't explain what she had done though, which I suppose didn't surprise me. Laura joined in and said she could do them too. She has special coaching to try to get her into a private girl's school when she is eleven.

But the odd thing was that I had been doing some mental maths with them that day and both girls, and several of the rest of the class, had real difficulty in multiplying numbers by 10! The other thing several children couldn't do was subtract 159 from 332 in their heads. They all wanted to write it down in the standard way! You would expect them to have more strategies than that for a relatively simple subtraction.

Laura and Karen are average ability nine-year-olds and should certainly have been able to cope with that level of computation mentally. They asked if they could write the subtraction down and I let them to see what they would do. All the children wrote it in the standard vertical form.

I asked a few children to tell me what they were doing. The said 'cross out the 3 and put a 1'. When I asked Laura and Karen why they had done that they did not know. Several others had the same problem. They could give no reason other than saying they were 'borrowing'.

Laura did this,
$$\begin{array}{r} 332 \\ -\ 159 \\ \hline 227 \end{array}$$
and Karen did this,
$$\begin{array}{r} 33\overset{1}{2} \\ 159 \\ \hline 253 \end{array}$$

and several other children made errors which indicated that they were not thinking about what the problem meant, and certainly not understanding it.

I get the general feeling that maths for them is more about learning *how to do something*, than about *understanding*.

'Laura isn't stretched enough'

Laura's mother often complains that her daughter 'isn't stretched enough', which worries me because Laura finds her work quite difficult! In the maths scheme she is clearly doing work that she does not really understand. Lots of the earlier stages seem to be missing. She lurches from page to page, constantly at my side asking 'How do I do this page?', 'Is it an add?', or 'Is it a sharing?'. It seems to me that despite all the 'pushing', many of these children actually achieve at a far lower level than I think they would if they were shown how to understand it first.

If I do the first few with Laura she is fine and goes away and repeats what I have shown her, but on a page of mixed problems she is all over the place. Today, Laura was trying to do some decimals. She was completely clueless about what 1.25 actually meant, so really I should take her back to earlier ideas. I can't take her off the scheme though because it is school policy that we do it in the junior department, and I do realise that with the National Curriculum, I need something as a structure, but as I'm such a young teacher I feel I have to keep quiet about my reservations about the scheme.

What can I do?

I am planning 'activity' maths twice a week and am integrating investigational things into that to try to build up confidence and understanding.

Sharing out the biscuits

I decided to start with sharing biscuits. It proved very successful. I made all the children wash their hands, and then got them to sit around tables in friendship groups. I said no group was to be smaller than 3 or larger than 6. I put a clean piece of paper on each table and put some biscuits on it so that each group had something that would take a while.

I said they had to divide out the biscuits fairly between everyone in the group and they were not to eat anything until they had done that and I had seen it and talked to them about it. I would then let them eat the biscuits, after which they were to draw a picture of what they had done in their group.

Some of the children who seemed from their book work to understand division and fractions got very confused. James said that 11 biscuits shared between 3 was 2 and 2 left over. The others wanted to share out the odd biscuits but he said it was 'a remainder' and they were to leave it. He can usually do maths really easily – he's on book 7 of the scheme, but he didn't want to admit that he was not sure what to do with those two biscuits!

It was fascinating how each group recorded what they had done differently. Figure 17.1 was typical of several children's work. They were quite unable to put down on paper what they had done. These two children had 9 biscuits between 2 of them. Figure 17.2 was also fairly typical of several children's work. This way of showing sharing is used in the text book. I thought it strange that this group of average-ability boys were unable to work out 21 biscuits shared between 5. They kept saying it was 5 each when I talked to them, but they had 5 pieces, not 5 whole ones.

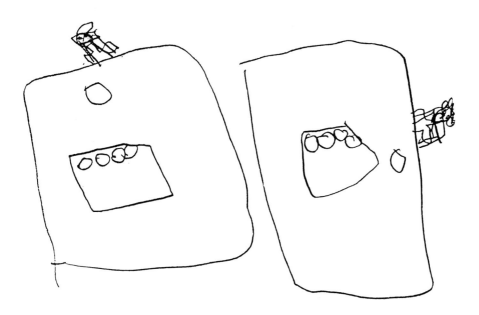

Figure 17.1

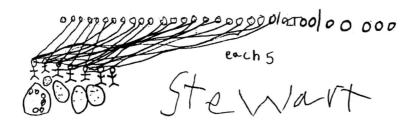

each 5

Stewart

Figure 17.2

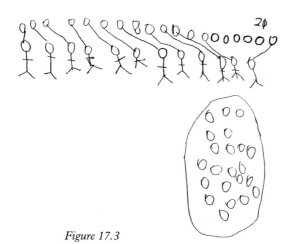

2¢

Figure 17.3

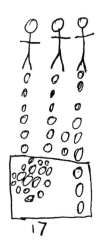

17

I started 17

Figure 17.4

Figure 17.3 on the previous was again an attempt to follow the methods of the text book. This child, and 12 others like him, could work it out with the biscuits, but he could not make sense of it on paper. I kept suggesting that he try a different method, but I noticed with lots of them that they thought they had to do it the 'right' way, the text book way.

Figure 17.4 shows how this group progressed. They first drew 17 biscuits, shared between 3 was 6 each. Then followed some fascinating discussion during which they worked out that it was 5 and two-thirds each.

Figure 17.5 shows 29 biscuits shared between 6 girls. They were fine on naming a half, but it broke down beyond this. The conversations of this group were remarkable as they tried to work it out to be totally fair. At one point they suggested that I could have some biscuit to have with my coffee as that would make the sharing easier! I thought this rather resourceful of them but politely declined.

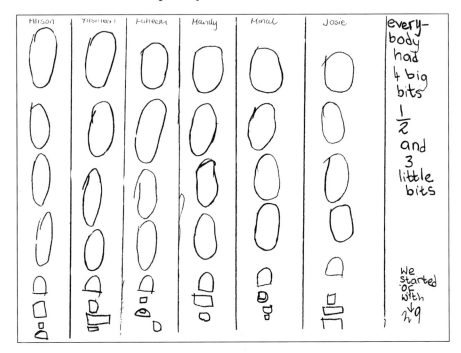

Figure 17.5

Conclusion

I think if I try to do this sort of maths about twice a week I will be giving the children some very good experiences which they wouldn't get just from the scheme. The discussions about the biscuits were the best bit. Just by looking at their recording you cannot see *the way* they arrived at what they did – the process of the thinking and all the talking. It was brilliant – the kids loved it and I definitely think that their work on fractions and division is improving.

$-18-$ Do they <u>really</u> know how to do it?
Shirley Clarke

Age	9–11
Situation	advisory teacher with a group
Maths	multiplication/problem solving
Theme	bright, text book taught children struggle with a task

In the previous chapter we saw how, although Jenny did not have much experience, she intuitively knew that, despite being well drilled in text book methods, the children seemed to have something missing from their understanding. In this chapter Shirley Clarke recounts a similar experience.

A teacher I was working with had spent half a term on multiplication working from a text book with his nine- and ten-year-olds. They could do long multiplication – the lot – and knew how to use all the four rules: division, subtraction etc. So where should he go from here? He asked me to take his two brightest children and to extend them. I set the two boys, Patrick and Andrew, a problem, to see how many 2p coins would cover the top of their table. I expected that they might use their multiplication knowledge in this situation. The fact that they did not seem to see that the problem involved multiplication flabbergasted their teacher. In the end, they proved to themselves that multiplication is repeated addition, but reading this account you will see why knowledge of text book multiplication seemed to leave these bright children with the inability to solve a simple problem.

I gave the boys three 2p coins, and asked how many would cover their table top (a standard half-metre table). Their agreed estimate was 175. Ten minutes later they had produced the work illustrated on the next page in Figure 18.1. By 'jumping' each 2p coin over, they had found how many fitted along each side. After some discussion Patrick asked for a calculator and put in 19 × 40, while Andrew did the sums shown overleaf in Figure 18.2.

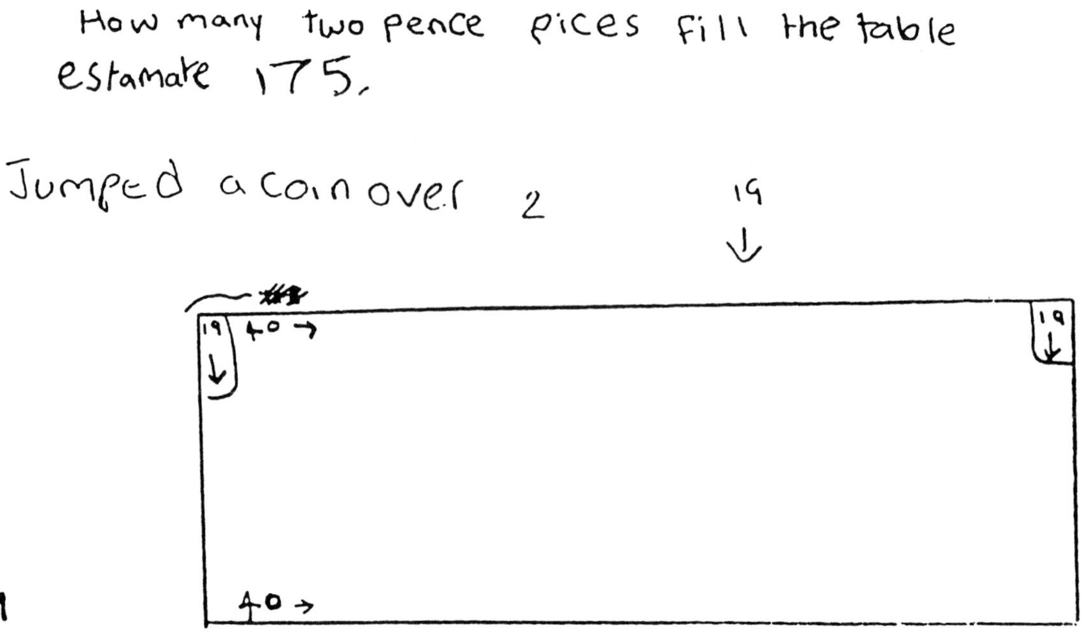

How many two pence pices fill the table
estamate 175.

Jumped a coin over 2   19
                                ↓

Figure 18.1

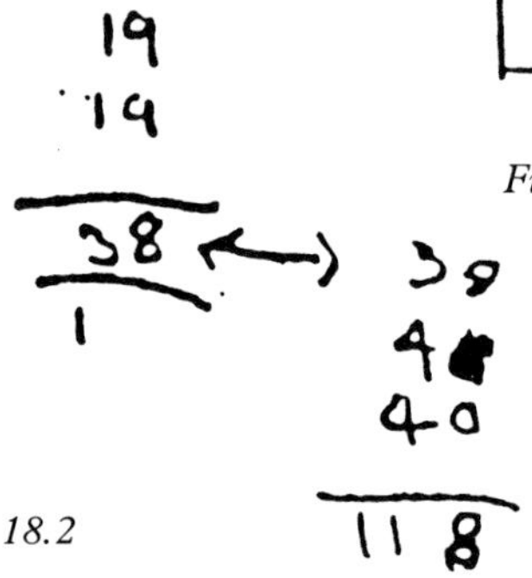

19
·19
───
38 ←→ 39
1   4⬛
       4·0
       ───
       11 8

Figure 18.2

I asked how they were getting on. 'I thought 19×40 would be how many go all round the edge, but it's not. Andrew's made it 118.'

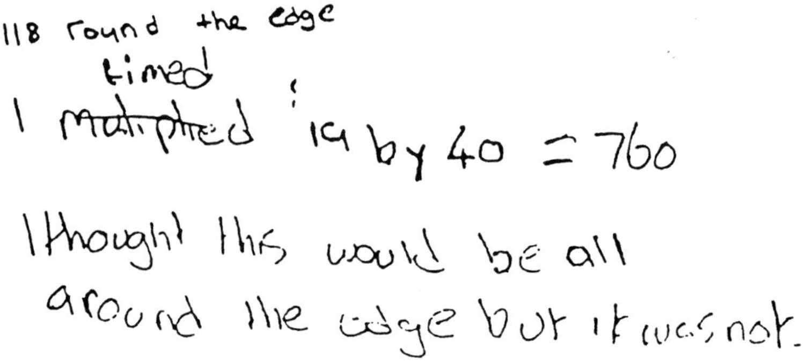

118 round the edge
        timed
I matiptied 19 by 40 = 760

I thought this would be all around the edge but it was not.

Figure 18.3

'We've got how many go round the edge, so now we're going to work out how many go all round inside that, then the line all round inside that and so on until we've covered the table.' (see Figure 18.3)

```
188.
114
110
 96
 92
 88
 84
 80
 76
 72
 68

 64

 60
 56  ·5
 52
 48
 44
 40
 36
 32
─────
1304
```

I took 4 away from the last result.

Figure 18.4

They decided the next 'perimeter' would be 4 less than the first 'because there are 4 corners.' A long list of these was made, 4 subtracted from each number, then totalled on the calculator. See Figure 18.4.

The boys were not happy with this result. 'It can't be that many.' I suggested they find another way of solving the problem so they could check the answer (Figure 18.5).

we got a metre stick & mesured the table.

Figure 18.5

Having done this, they sat blankly staring at the table and the metre stick. More discussion together and they wrote (Figure 18.6):

we need to find a different method to make sure it is right.

Figure 18.6

Large sheets of paper were requested, which they taped to the table. They drew a line along the bottom of the table, the width of a coin. A second line was then drawn along the side of the table, also the width of a coin. I imagined this would be continued until they could count all the squares, but they seemed dissatisfied with this method. They wrote (Figure 18.7):

we coverd the desk with paper and drew squaes on it but it did not work because the lines wouldn't go strait and the paper was not completly covering the table.

Figure 18.7

125

For the next five minutes the boys entered various sums into the calculator. (Figure 18.8)

$$19 \div 40 \qquad 40 \div 19 \qquad 40 \times 19$$

Figure 18.8

They seemed to have an instinct for the numbers they needed, but no clear idea of what they should do with them or why. They began to look distressed, then told me they were stuck. Their feelings were that they had lots of answers but didn't know which was right. I asked if they could tell me how they would place the coins on the table if they had lots. They said they would go all round the edge, then inside that, then inside that and so on, still obviously committed to this method of covering the table. I asked if there was a different way they could place the coins. After much thinking Patrick said, 'In rows' and then from both Patrick and Andrew a second later 'I think I've got it now'. Another list of numbers appeared. (Figure 18.9)

40
39
40
39
40
39
40
39
40
39

Figure 18.9

Figure 18.10

'The first row has 40, the next 39, then 40, then 39 etc.' they explained. 'If you put coins exactly on top of one another they leave a big gap, but if you put the coin above in between the two you cover more space.' See Figure 18.10. They then decided (Figure 18.11):

We are going to count rows and we decided to use the most amount of paper as possible. The first row has 40 in it the next row has 39 in it. *Figure 18.11*

But how many rows of 40 and 39? This was the next dilemma. They decided it probably would be more than 19 because you may have space at the top of the table for another line. There seemed to be no way of finding this out without lots of coins, so a decision was made to go back to coins on top of one another. A list of 19–40s appeared. Andrew dictated the string of 40s while Patrick entered them in the calculator. This proved to be disastrous, as they keep losing one another, and had to restart. After three attempts they abandoned the calculator and combined pairs of 40s to make 80s, then pairs of 80s to make 160s, with an 80 and

126

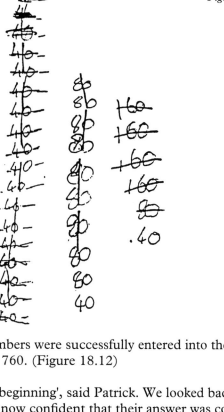

Figure 18.12

a 40 left over. These numbers were successfully entered into the
calculator with a total of 760. (Figure 18.12)

'That's what I did at the beginning', said Patrick. We looked back at what
he had done. They were now confident that their answer was correct and
told me they had added up 19 40s. 'And 19 × 40 is the same', said
Patrick. They had proved to themselves that multiplication is repeated
addition! (Figure 18.13)

We . thought that 175 would be the amant of coins
it was. But it wasi'nt. it was. 760 and we found that
175 was about ¼ a quarter of the table.

760 2p equles £5.20p

We wanted to no how much money 760 2-penses . is

760 × 2 = 1520 pense = £ 15.20p

Figure 18.13

'I wonder how much money that is' said Andrew. After asking them to
write a comment about their work, I left them to it.

This article first appeared in *Investigator*, a newspaper devoted to promoting an
investigative and problem solving approach to the teaching of mathematics. *Investigator* is
published through SMILE, and this article is reproduced here with kind permission of the
SMILE Centre. For more information about *Investigator* and other SMILE publications,
contact the SMILE Centre, Isaac Newton Centre for Professional Development,
Lancaster Road, London W11.

−19− Teachers talk about schemes
(a) Staffroom conversation – *Two middle school teachers*
(b) Teaching maths without relying on a scheme – *Moira Proudfoot*

A Staffroom conversation

Age	all ages
Situation	two teachers talking
Maths	fractions; multiplication; division; written problems; investigations.
Themes	the advantages and disadvantages of working from a scheme; the need to keep maths active

Two teachers who work in a middle school, where maths is taught mainly from a scheme feel that the advantages of having some sort of scheme are often lost by teachers wanting to work the system where 'every child works at their own pace'. This is what they said:

- It sounds right – children working at their own pace, but it hides many problems.

- Children queue endlessly – so many are stuck that it is almost impossible to cope and you end up giving inadequate explanations so that you can deal with all the waiting children.

- Maths stops being something active and tends to become more passive with an emphasis on 'doing the page' rather than understanding the concept.

- The importance of language and the use of apparatus can tend to get lost using a scheme.

- Children ask questions that require in-depth explanations. I jotted down every question I was asked in a space of five minutes this morning. Six questions were about classroom administration, and five were about the content of the maths.

These five were:

1 Anna just did not understand her page of fractions. It was the third time she had been up to me. She could not see how to colour $\frac{3}{4}$ red and $\frac{1}{4}$ blue. Then she had to write $\frac{3}{4} + \frac{1}{4} = 1$.

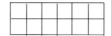

Colour $\frac{3}{4}$ red

and $\frac{1}{4}$ blue

Write $\frac{3}{4} + \frac{1}{4} = 1$

2 I could not answer Anna in any depth because I was working with David who could not see how to do a subtraction with Dienes, because he could not understand exchange. He thought the act of exchanging was part of what he was taking away.

3 Shakoar said 'I can't do these kind of sums. Are they times?'

$$4\overline{)0.96 \text{ m}}$$

$$5\overline{)6.80 \text{ m}}$$

4 Brian came up and asked 'What does this word say?' pointing to 'tessellate'. I explained quickly, then he went off and I could see that the was trying to do a tessellation with circles.

5 Elizabeth could not understand a 'problems' page. She had more or less successfully done four pages of subtractions but when it came to problems embedded in words she was totally unable to cope.

- That was all in five minutes. You can guess the sorts of replies that I was giving. I was saying how to do it, not explaining what it meant.

- I spent a lot of the rest of the lesson with Elizabeth trying to sort out what the questions meant. I sat by her. Of course there was a constant stream of questions from other children but at least I sorted Elizabeth out.

- Minal will be on that page soon. It would make much more sense to have these children in groups so that our efforts were being used more economically.

The two biggest weaknesses of this system

1 It is a waste of teacher time.

2 The children are not understanding in depth. (On a fractions section, you just about get a child understanding when the next page is shape. It would make much more sense to go on with fractions so that you obtained deep understanding.)

The advantages of a scheme	1 The children work on their own and free you to do other things (theoretically).
	2 You have a structure to the maths which you need if you are not a maths specialist.
	3 You hope that the bright children are catered for.

What can you do in a school where you must use a scheme?

The big question seems to be: How can you take the advantages of a scheme and make it work better in the classroom? Some teachers think it is better to see the scheme as back-up. Some would rather do some whole class work – there are lots of starting points that all abilities can cope with. Some think it is possible to link that to ability group work for some of the time.

Conclusion

- A scheme is a tool, not the master.
- Schemes can help to ensure that children follow a progression.
- They give practice in computation.
- Used *after* activities, they help to consolidate concepts.
- Used well they can build up confidence.
- Used badly they put the emphasis on 'doing the page' rather than the maths
- Used badly they can make maths into a solitary and silent activity when it should be a 'doing and talking' activity.

B   Teaching maths without relying on a scheme

Age	7–11
Situation	teaching head
Maths	investigations and setting tasks verbally
Themes	'real ' maths without using a scheme; helping children to develop their own methods

Moira is a head with a full teaching commitment. She writes here about her experiences during a year on secondment, and also of her work with seven- to eleven-year-olds in Primary Schools.

I have always enjoyed all forms of mathematics. During my schooling I was fortunate to have maths teachers who believed in allowing their pupils to work from first principles rather than by rote learning. We worked out tables for ourselves, saw the repetition, and then learned the significant numbers. Thus it was natural for me in my own teaching to consider presenting maths to children without using a scheme.

Not all teachers appreciate that this is 'real' maths. While on secondment, I spent many hours with a class of eight to nine-year-olds. I remember being delighted with the children's work. They had been thinking for themselves and I was pleased with their progress. When their teacher came back to take over her class, I heard her say 'Now it's time for *real* maths: get out your work cards and maths books.' I had a good laugh about this but I feel that this shows up a considerable problem. Many headteachers, teachers, governors, parents and even children see maths as something that comes out of a text book. This is a very false and narrow view of maths. Personally, I don't think you can do maths justice if you just work from a scheme because:

- it makes it boring;

- it can show only one aspect of maths – the content – but we must go for the processes too – the thinking; and

- children are held up if they cannot read the page in the scheme, but if you toss out ideas, it's all verbal and the child who is slow to read but mathematically able can do very well and develop a positive attitude to maths.

In one school where I taught children aged between nine and eleven, the children came to me from a class where maths had been taught rigidly from a scheme. I found many of them had a very negative approach to maths. I tried to interest them by putting investigations in boxes around the edge of the room. When their other work had been finished, they could then choose an investigation. This element of choice helped to create a more positive feeling in the class. The children enjoyed the activities, and often became so involved that it led to class discussions. Gradually the children realised that often the maths problem/investigation had many answers – not only one right answer. For example, there are numerous ways of costing a residential visit, a class picnic, and a tuck shop for sports day. All would provide reinforcement of the four rules of number, and be much more exciting than a page of sums.

Gradually, as the children got used to this more open-ended way of working, and the idea that there often is no one right answer, I began to integrate investigations into the maths within the classroom. This formed a base for mathematical topics which did not rely on a scheme.

As a teaching head in a village school, I still use investigations as a start to a topic. I also have a couple of afternoons a week when I toss out ideas to the children. During a discussion, they are encouraged to voice their ideas before working practically on the problem. I try to get *them* thinking. So, for example, I might ask them what they think will happen when they throw two dice – will any numbers come up more than the others? When they have said what they think will happen they have to say *how much evidence they will need to prove their point*. So in this case the question would be how often would they need to throw the dice to prove their point?

If I was doing shape with seven-year-olds, I would ask them to tell me which of the shapes they think might tessellate. Which shapes would they use to cover a floor? If they think triangles, I would ask, 'Will any triangle tessellate?' 'What about circles?' If they say they will not tessellate, I ask, 'How could they adapt the circle? What could they add or take away from the circle?' I have used this way of working with children from about age seven, and I think that they enjoy maths enormously working in this way.

Why I use investigations

- Investigations tend to reinforce maths skills that the children have already learnt.

- They create situations in which you can clearly see what a child can do, and how far they understand it. They are good guides to a child's level of knowledge, and help the teacher with assessment and future plans.

- They provide starting points for a child to explore. It stops maths just being about right and wrong.

- It makes maths fun.

- It emphasises the child's own method. For example, James uses a rather slow process for multiplication (see Figure 19.1). Although I will help him to make his method quicker, at the moment he is secure with this method. It is *his* method, *his* thinking.

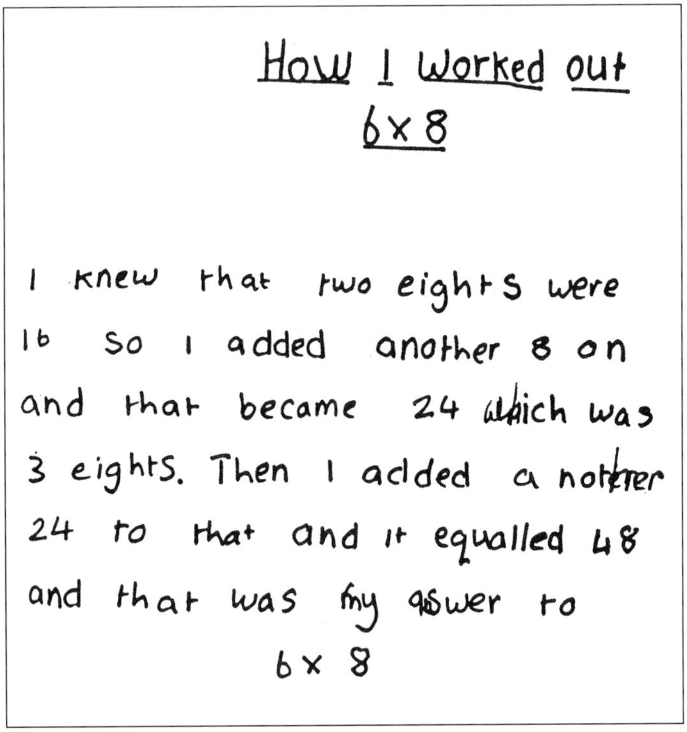

> ## How I Worked out
> ## 6 × 8
>
> I knew that two eights were 16 so I added another 8 on and that became 24 which was 3 eights. Then I added another 24 to that and it equalled 48 and that was my aswer to
> ## 6 × 8

Figure 19.1 James' method of multiplication

This emphasis on the relevance of maths and allowing children to develop their own methods is basic to my approach. By giving the thinking over to the children in this way, they become much more ready to use their own methods and become secure and confident with maths.

−20− I'll do it my way
Sue Atkinson

A   Rachel explains her method

Age	9–11
Situation	individual in class
Maths	subtraction/place value
Theme	children's own methods

Rachel (aged eleven) was fed up being told by her teachers that she did her subtractions 'wrong'. She complained at home of being told off and told to 'start with the units'. When asked to explain her method for 372 take 187, Rachel said, 'I start with the hundreds. I wouldn't write this one down, it's too easy, I would just do it in my head. It's 372 take off 100 that's 272, take off 80 is 192, then take off 7 leaves 185.' (see Figure 20.1).

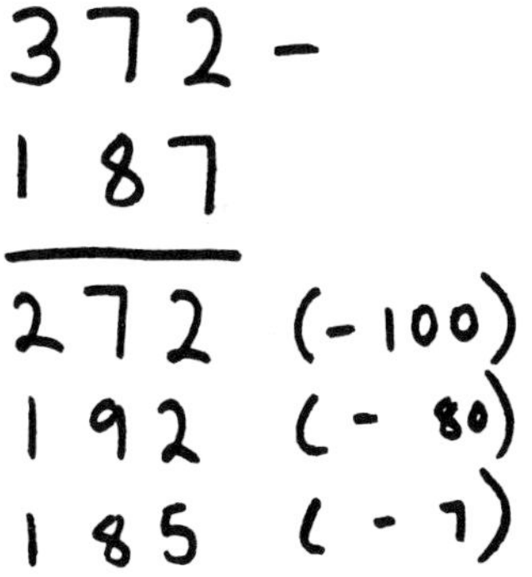

$$
\begin{array}{ll}
372\ - & \\
187 & \\
\hline
272 & (-100) \\
192 & (-80) \\
185 & (-7) \\
\end{array}
$$

Figure 20.1

$$
\begin{array}{l}
20013 \\
\ \ 4975 \\
\hline
16013 \\
15113 \\
15043 \\
15038 \\
\end{array}
$$

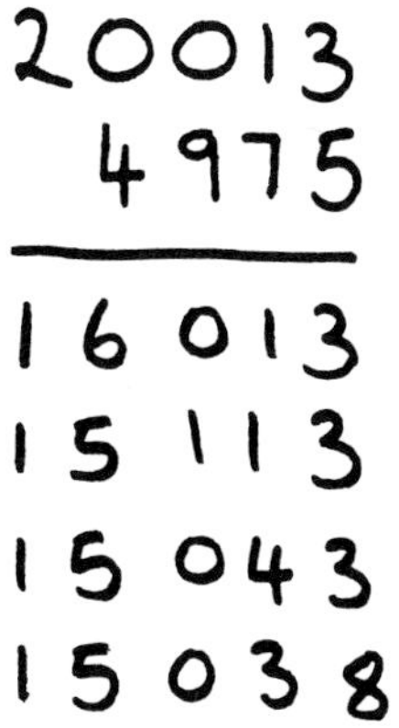

Figure 20.2

When asked to explain a harder one she wrote the sum shown in Figure 20.2. It is the same as her mental method i.e. she first subtracts the 4000, then the 900 etc.

B   Alex explains what she does

Age   9–11
Situation individual in class
Maths   subtraction/place value
Theme   children's own methods

Alex   I take a hundred, so that leaves 2, so that gives me 17, I have to take one of those and make this 12, then I take 7 from 12 is 5, 8 from 16 is 8 and 1 from 2 is 1.

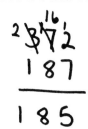

Figure 20.3

Adult   What were you really doing when you were crossing out the 17 and putting 16?
Alex   I was taking a ten from the 17 tens and exchanging it into 10 units so that I had enough units to take away the 7. (see Figure 20.3.)

C   Sabrena records in her own way

Age   7–9
Situation individual in class
Maths   problem solving
Theme   children's own methods of recording

Sabrena (aged eight) was calculating how much milk we would need for our three-day residential visit. She was well below average in her maths attainment, but found this problem quite easy to solve, despite the fact that it used maths at quite a difficult level for her.

She brought a cereal bowl and a pint milk bottle in from home, and worked out that one pint was enough for five bowls of cereal. Her recording (Figure 20.4) shows how she worked out how much milk was needed for three days. Her recording shows a mixture of types of tallies; it was entirely her own invented method.

Another child worked out that six pints of milk would be needed over the three days for cups of tea. Then Sabrena set about finding out how much all the milk would cost at 21p per pint.

At first Sabrena was confused with her piles of plastic money, but then she put it out in sets of 21p, two 10p coins and one 1p coin. She then

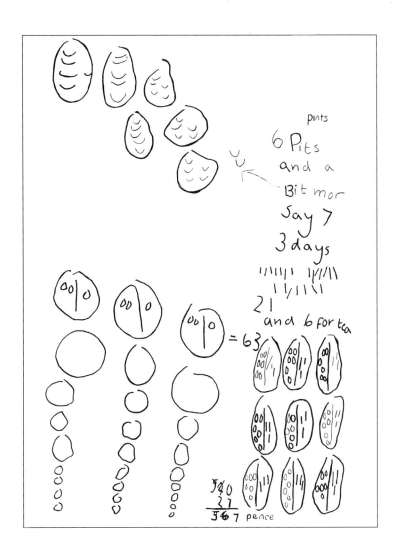

Figure 20.4

started to record her work (Figure 20.4) because, she said, 'I might forget what I have done'. She could see a real need to record. Then she said, 'This is too much drawing' and shorthanded her method by drawing sets of 63p. I was impressed at her place value understanding.

This use of sets became a strong feature of Sabrena's maths, and other children in the class adapted it whenever they needed to multiply. It was fairly easy, a few months after this, to develop Sabrena's multiplication skills using her own recording as a sound basis. She was soon able to multiply securely.

−21− Real 'real problem-solving'
Owen Tregaskis

Age	9–11
Situation	whole class
Maths	'real' problem solving
Theme	the effectiveness of maths teaching from real problems

In this chapter, Owen Tregaskis looks at real problem solving in school and describes a project undertaken by him in a junior classroom.

The term 'real problem solving' has been introduced to primary schools but has a wide range of meanings. To some teachers a 'word problem' is considered as being 'real' even though it has no relevance to the children (e.g. Tom has £2 to spend. How many 35p bars of chocolate can he buy?) It reflects the children's lives, but is not personal to them. To many other teachers questions like 'Where is the best site for a local airport' is considered real, but here again children are not personally concerned with the outcome. These types of problems or simulations are a vital part of our maths teaching but I want to argue that they need to be seen as additional to real problem solving which involves children's *real* lives and actually brings some change to those lives.

I want to describe a real problem which was solved by a group of children, and then outline some ideas about real problem solving in our classrooms. (This problem-solving work owes much to the Open University course 'Mathematics Across the Curriculum'.)

Sports day

I asked my class of 32 nine- to eleven-year-olds for ideas to improve the school. The ideas ranged from 'Burn it down' to 'Longer playtimes' and 'Swimming every day'. Many children suggested a sports day and this seemed the most popular suggestion, so our real problem solving project was born. Over the next month the children worked on this problem using some of the maths lessons, but mainly playtimes and odd moments during the day. The children had the satisfaction of solving a problem and seeing how maths could help to produce a more satisfactory solution. The main differences in this real problem solving and those outlined above are in the ownership of the problem and the role of the teacher. This was a problem which was about the children's own lives and, when solved, one which would change their lives.

Role of the teacher

The traditional role of the teacher is to set children problems, dictate the method of solution and then tell the children if they got the right answer. In real problem solving the teacher's role is one of helper or facilitator. The teacher helps children to clarify what the problem is and supports children's efforts at finding solutions. The answer is correct if the children agree that it works in practice

In this instance, the children organised and ran a very successful sports day, which therefore means that they came up with the right answers. Right from the initial brianstorming sessions, the teacher had to take a role which helped the children to solve the problem but not input any ideas. Most importantly I felt that I must not veto such ideas as 'motor-bike scrambling', or 'horse racing', because such a veto would take the problem away from the children. On the day of the sports I gave myself the role of photographer and was far too busy to solve any problems for the children.

The teacher, therefore, is vital in order to give the children the necessary mathematical skills and to help them develop social skills.

Mathematical skills

The children had used the skills of brainstorming and sorting ideas by creating a topic web before this particular project, but they were now given a real situation in which to practise these skills. After about one week of working in sub-groups, each sub-group working on one branch of our topic web, I felt that the children were getting frustrated because of lack of experience in organising a sports day. I then stepped in and proposed a 'mini-sports day' which would last for ten minutes one playtime and have very simple refreshments. This is really the mathematical process of simplification used in a practical situation.

The group working on refreshments were given plenty of practice in the traditional arithmetic and graph-making skills. A survey of local shops had been made and it was established that the cheapest way to buy crisps was to buy a box of 48 packets. The problem was to decide which flavour to buy. Catherine made a graph of the children's favourite flavours (Figure 21.1). From this graph Catherine found that the favourite was 'sausage and tomato'. Unfortunately, Catherine did not like sausage and tomato and what is more, she suspected that other children did not like them as well. She tried another survey: 'Do you like sausage and tomato crisps?' She found out that eight children did not like sausage and tomato. Try again. 'Which crisps do you not like?' Here, Catherine gives everyone two chances to name flavours that they do not like (Figure 21.2). The result is a graph to show that sausage and tomato flavour is the favourite, but also the most disliked. Bacon flavoured crisps are the least disliked and so this is the flavour to buy. Catherine, and the rest of the class have learnt that the most important thing about carrying out a survey and making a graph is to ask the right questions.

Figure 21.1

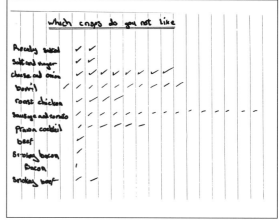

Figure 21.2

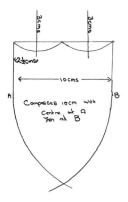

Figure 21.3

The group concerned with the prizes decided to make a shield for the winning team. The problem came when they wanted to draw the curves at the bottom. I suggested that a book on heraldry might help. They found out how to use a pair of compasses to draw the curves (Figure 21.3). Later on, when the group working on drawing out the course for the races wanted to make a staggered start, I sent them to see how the prizes group had solved the problem of drawing a shield. Both groups began to realise the usefulness of drawing arcs to produce a line or series of points at a constant distance from a given point. Imagine the delight of the children, when the groundsmen came to mark out the course, to see adults using the same method that they had invented for themselves (Figure 21.4).

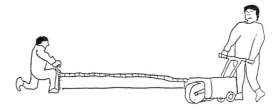

Figure 21.4

138

The groundmen, on the other hand, were a little put out by the children's request for a running track of 37 metres. Twenty-five or 50 metres made sense, but why 37? The children had been concerned that everyone should have a fair chance in the race so the slowest runner had been asked to run as fast as possible for as long as possible. This distance was 37 metres and so, to be fair to everyone, this had to be the distance of the race. Once again, the important thing about maths is the question you ask in the first place.

The pricing of the refreshments caused a few problems in arithmetic. Much experiment and long division was required to prove that more profit could be made if sweets were bought in large packets and repackaged for sale than if the children made their own sweets. Frances (a good mathematician) produced a very elegant long division sum to

Francis Method

We bought a box of 48 packets of crisps for £3-20. We wanted to know how much to for our crisps.

I divided £3-20 by 48 like this

```
        6+0.6+0.6
  48 )  320
        288      (6 × 48)
         32
         28.8    (0.6 × 48)
          3.2
          2.88   (0.06 × 48)
           .32
```

Each packet of Crisps will cost 6.66p.

Figure 21.5

Anna's Method

I thought that in Martin's we pay 9p for a packet of crisps.

If we ask the children to pay 9p we will get 9×48=432p so we would make £4-32−£3-20= £1=12p profit.

WE could charge 8p for a Packet of crisps which would give us 8×48=384p. We would still make 384−320 = 64p profit and all the children would be happy because they would have cheap crisps.

Figure 21.6

find what we must charge for a packet of crisps (Figure 21.5). She came up with the answer of 6.666p and did not know what to do with the answer. Anna, not such a sophisticated mathematician used trial and error to produce a much more understandable answer (see Figure 21.6).

Language and social skills

Although the children were working in groups to solve parts of the problem, I brought the class together to enable each decision to be agreed by the whole class. This gave the children plenty of practice in putting forward arguments and in voting. Many of the debates became heated and we became involved in looking at various methods of voting (multiple votes, transferable votes and especially when a vote became really important, secret voting). The writing of rules for some of the games stretched the children's writing skills, especially as the rules had to be written for the parents (who were invited to act as starters, judges etc.). Cooks and dinner ladies were pressed into acting as readers, to make sure that the rules could be understood before they were printed and sent out to parents.

Real problem solving and the National Curriculum

The National Curriculum states that pupils should use maths in real life problems. The Non-statutory Guidance, which has been written to provide a reference for teachers in planning and implementing the National Curriculum, tells us how important employers see the need to teach children how to use their maths effectively. The Guidance continues to suggest that applying maths does not come easily to many pupils and, 'For this reason, pupils, at all stages, need to have experience of tackling "real life" problems as an integral part of their experience of mathematics.' (Non-statutory Guidance, National Curriculum Council, 1989 D4, Section 2.2.)

Finally

This was a major project spread over many weeks, but real problem solving need not be on such a large scale. There are many classroom tasks involved with storage, tidiness, ease of access etc. which can be tackled in a single afternoon. I have found it important to involve the whole class as this ensures that more mathematical skills are introduced. Last year, while working with a class of ten-year-old children, we worked on the scissor problem. Each group of children discussed and produced a list of uses of the scissors and problems of storage, care etc. The whole class voted on the order of importance of the problems. Back in groups, solutions were suggested and these voted on by the whole class.

Larger problems can involve parties, educational visits, assemblies or activities at playtime. The most important aspect to create in the classroom is an atmosphere of awareness of the problems around us and confidence on the part of the children so that they can solve the problems. If the children are finding solutions difficult, they know that the teacher is there to help them with techniques but will not provide suggestions as to possible solutions.

−22− Does maths with reason work?
Nick James

Age	9–11
Situation	advisory teacher with a class
Maths	fractions
Theme	attainment in maths, maths with reason tested over time

Throughout this book we have shown how children can achieve at high levels when they are taught in a way that makes maths have a reason, and where doing *and* talking *comes before* recording.

Here, Nick James tells the story of two girls he worked with when making the Video for the Open University Course 'Developing Mathematical Thinking'. The story now has a fascinating sequel because Kelly became the first woman engineer to graduate from her college – a real success story for a child who was failing in her education.

The girls, Kelly and Samantha, both then aged nine, were in a classroom where do, talk *and* record *was the basic framework for their learning of maths. The class was doing a topic on fractions, and had worked on several specific examples of activities that embodied the concepts involved in the naming and equivalence of fractions. This was done so that they would gradually develop a growing awareness of the underlying sameness of the concepts.*

One morning, Kelly came to school really mad.

'We had sausages last night for tea! There are five of us in the family and there were eight sausages in the packet. Do you know what Dad did?! He gave us one sausage each, then he cut the remaining three into halves, gave us one half each and… then he ate the remaining half!'

Clearly she had another view of how to share out the sausages! This was the problem we watched Kelly and Samantha solve on the video extract.

Figure 22.1 shows Kelly's record of her solution; an operation which Samantha performed on eight sausages on a plate nearby.

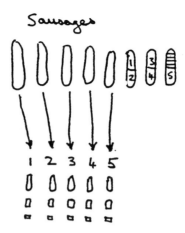

*Figure 22.1 Kelly's record of how she would share out
eight sausages between five people*

There is nothing particularly remarkable about this drawing until you listen to the discussion which followed between the two girls and their teacher, Geoff Adams.

'One of these little pieces is one fifth of half a sausage.'
'That's a tenth of a whole sausage, because the other half could be cut into ten as well!'
'Yeah!... so one-fifth of half a sausage is the same as one-tenth of a whole one!'

This was particularly interesting because nobody had ever spoken to these girls about multiplication of fractions, but they seemed so secure about the naming of fractions that the above truth was self-evident. And what about this next conversation? ... all the more surprising since addition of fractions, improper fractions and the notion of lowest common denominator had, likewise, never been explicitly mentioned!

'So each person gets one whole sausage, a half of a sausage and a tenth.'
'That's one whole and six tenths... so each person gets sixteen tenths!... of one sausage.'

As if that's not enough, Samantha suddenly announces:

'This (a fifth of half a sausage) is a sixtieth of the whole packet because there are six sausages in the packet. Oh no... it's one-eighteenth because there are eight sausages and each one is cut into ten pieces.'

Nobody in the class has ever looked at fractions like 'eightieths'. Their concept of naming fractions is being transferred to a novel situation. Later the girls go on to explain that...

'... each person gets one whole, five-eightieths and one-eightieth of the whole packet of sausages... that's sixteen-eightieths each!'

And this is all the more remarkable when I tell you that the head teacher was just about to have Kelly and Samantha referred to special schools because they had 'learning difficulties!' He had to go immediately and withdraw all the paperwork he had done!

Two years later, I was in the same classroom as Kelly. We were, for some reason which escapes me now, trying to find a fifth of ninety-five. Said one pupil, 'Oh you need to split ninety-five into fives!' 'No you don't,' said Kelly, 'You have to split it into five!' The teacher and I then stood at the side of the class for the next thirty minutes whilst Kelly proceeded to convince the class why it was splitting ninety-five into five and not fives.

Only the letter 's' separates the two statements. The answer is the same in both cases, but there is a world of difference in the actual processes being used ... only Kelly's process is correct in this context. Setting the mathematical niceties aside for the moment, the significant thing about this anecdote is Kelly's retention of the concept. How often have you found yourself saying, only a few weeks after spending considerable time in class on a particular concept, 'But we've just done the naming of fractions! Can't you remember?' or, at the start of a new academic year, saying, 'Didn't last year's teacher do fractions with you?' Well, here is Kelly, two years down the line, and she still has all the confidence and clarity of understanding on the matter, not just to remember but also to convince all her peers.

The suggestion in the National Curriculum Proposals is (DES 1988) that the most able ten per cent of pupils might be expected to attain Level 6 or higher at age eleven. Yet these girls, thought by some at one stage to be low attainers and at the very opposite end of the ability spectrum, were achieving these levels at the age of nine plus. It's my experience that most fifteen-year-olds cannot operate with fractions like these nine-year-olds and certainly most pupils seem to need constant revision because retention is so low.

I therefore leave you with the wonderfully exciting possibility ... taught to work investigatively, as we've described it, and then encouraged to transfer these thinking strategies to the formation of concepts conventionally listed in syllabuses using programmes of study exemplified by do, talk and record activities, might not these below-average pupils in fact achieve Grade 1 in their exams? Will those low attainers not become high achievers? And what of any set of national criteria in the subject – given the teaching approaches explored here, might not the achievement of any attainment targets become purely academic?

This chapter is based on an extract from *Investigative Approaches to the Learning and Teaching of Mathematics*, an unpublished paper by Nick James.

$-23-$ Whole-school approaches to maths with reason
Sue Atkinson

Age	3–11
Situation	whole school working together
Maths	aspects of the entire curriculum
Theme	maths with reason as a whole school policy; working with parents; discussion starters

Here we look at how teachers have tried to work together to develop a whole-school approach to the teaching of maths. By 'whole -school approach' we mean a policy agreed by all the teachers, so that the approach to maths is consistent throughout the school. This policy is not static but in a continual state of revision and reformulation.

One of the many ways that schools can start to review their maths policy is to have some sort of maths event such as an evening meeting with parents, or a workshop session to make some games with both children and parents. One school had a teachers' meeting in which they brought every bit of maths apparatus out and looked at it to see what was there. It was found to be a source of renewed enthusiasm for practical maths. Other schools have other approaches and we will outline a few of them.

A small-scale maths activity afternoon

One school planned a maths afternoon before an evening meeting at which they were going to talk about their maths policy to the parents. Every teacher put out maths activities tables and every child did maths in some form or other throughout the afternoon.

For the younger children, aged between five and seven, the different apparatus that was available included:

- polydrons;
- interlocking cubes and other small construction apparatus and puzzles;
- Lego, including technical Lego and motors;
- bricks and other large construction toys;
- a table of playhouse material, designed to help children count, match and sort;
- games which involved shape, counting, logic, place value, money etc. and a variety of strategy games;
- water and sand trays for capacity work;
- sewing, cooking, woodwork; and
- role play within the playhouse, such as shopping (with paper and pencil for writing, and a calculator).

The older children, aged between seven and eleven, were split into three main groups. One group worked with the headteacher in the hall, using two computers, exploring number patterns, and working with LOGO. The two other groups had a variety of mathematical activities that the children were currently using as part of their on-going topic and maths work. These included:

- each child doing a detailed plan of a picture as the basis for a tapestry;
- sewing patchwork cushions using a variety of templates, squares, hexgons, etc.;
- scale drawings and maps;
- strategy games and other mathematical games;
- maths puzzles and investigations;
- working on a time-line as part of the historical aspects of the class topic; and
- various aspects of practical maths which were a part of the on-going work in the class, like finding the volume of 3-D shapes and gathering data for a database to be put into the computer.

Organisation for this maths afternoon was simple and the parents expressed how much it helped them to be able to observe and join in, then to talk about it in the evening discussions.

A large-scale maths afternoon

Another school planned a large-scale maths event to take place all afternoon throughout the whole school. Each class teacher planned with her children a few mathematical activities, and parents and ancillary staff were each allocated a group. Other advisory support teachers and students from a nearby training college, were brought in to help. Some of the activities involved the children all afternoon, while for others they took turns in groups.

1 One group made a chequerboard garden.

2 All the water trays were taken outside and different aspects of capacity and volume work, floating and sinking, and other science ideas were explored.

3 Several groups were engaged in cooking for the 'cafe'.

4 Others, helped by some parents, ran the cafe, providing refreshments throughout the afternoon taking and counting the money.

5 A local college lent computers and a turtle, and several groups worked on LOGO.

6 Children took it in turns to play calculator games.

7 In the hall, the PE apparatus was set out for groups of children to act out *Bears in the Night* (Berenstain and Berenstain, 1972). In this story words like 'under', 'around', 'over', 'through' and 'down' are explored in story form, thus making the mathematical words clearly understood.

8 Some children ran stalls, as in a fête, taking money in payment for games they had devised.

9 Some children had planned large-scale drawings and games on the playground drawn in chalk. During the afternoon, parents supervised them painting these in various colours.

10 In another room, a large selection of maths games were available for parents and children to play (many made by the children).

11 Some of the older children had puzzles and investigations to show to, and often dumbfound, parents.

12 In one room typical workcards and worksheets were laid out, along with appropriate apparatus.

Parents were invited to walk around the school, looking at the variety of maths activities going on, and to join in where appropriate. Each teacher had put up a small notice by each activity, explaining its mathematical content and value. Everyone enjoyed the afternoon, and it led to very interesting parent–teacher discussions about the maths curriculum.

Parents work with teachers

Making games for a 'maths library'

In several schools, parents have worked with teachers to produce mathematical games and activities which their children can borrow and take home. These games are kept in a library at school with a card-index system.

Schools which have operated this system find that children enjoy maths, and parents appreciate the amount of involvement it gives them with their child's learning. For the children, it helps to integrate school maths with home maths.

Maths gardens

Schools with space have found it very beneficial to build a 'garden' in which mathematical ideas can be explored in lesson time or at playtime. This might include concrete shapes, a small raised pond (for water investigations rather than fish), gutters set in concrete for testing speeds of boats, a pendulum, and various slopes and inclines for testing speeds of toy cars. This can be built in several stages (see Figure 23.1)

Maths trails

Trails can be as simple as sending children around the school to look for, say, rectangles, squares and triangles, or can be much more complex involving the local environment beyond the school grounds – the streets, shops, fields, houses, in fact anything that will involve the children in searching and observing. Some of the sorts of questions might include:

1 Name the shapes on the nursery climbing frame or in the structure of the school roof. Try to build this shape with a construction kit.

2 What is the height of the big tree? How could we find out?

3 Why does the shadow of the netball post move around? Does it move in the same way every day?

4 Which shops in the high street are used the most frequently?

5 Could we fit everyone in the whole school into the big yellow circle on the school playground? If not, could we draw a circle big enough?

School maths policies

School maths policies are often thought of as a written document, whereas often the real policy is what actually goes on in the classroom – often less to do with anything written, and more to do with *attitude*. It is

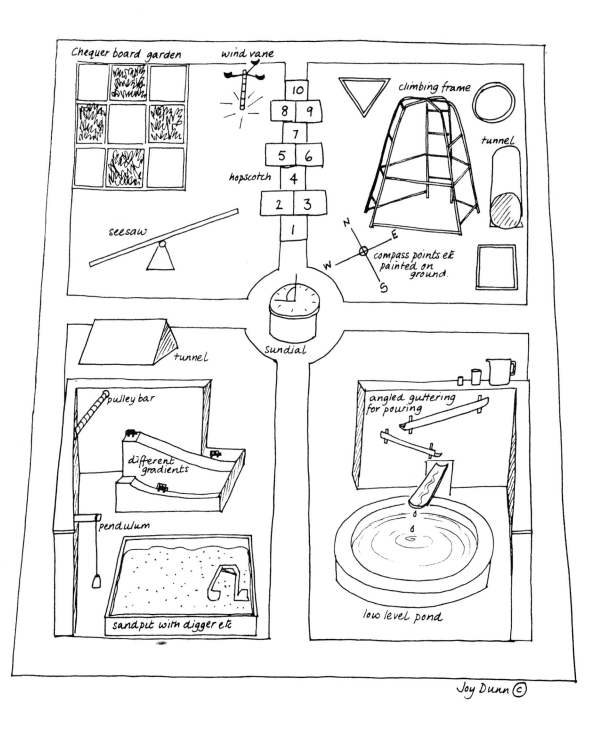

Figure 23.1 A maths garden

148

not so much *what* you teach, although of course this is important, it is *how* you teach it.

Headteachers and maths co-ordinators work with their colleagues and parents to set up a way of approaching maths within the school that will develop the crucial 'positive attitudes' (see Figure 23.2) as set out in the DES publication *Maths from 5–16*.

A FACTS

1. remembering terms
2. remembering notation
3. remembering conventions
4. remembering results

B SKILLS

5. performing basic operations
6. sensible use of calculator
7. simple practical skills in maths
8. ability to communicate maths
9. use of microcomputers in maths activity

C CONCEPTUAL STRUCTURES

10. understanding basic concepts
11. relationship between concepts
12. selecting appropriate data
13. using maths in context
14. interpreting results

D GENERAL MATHEMATICAL STRATEGIES

15. ability to estimate
16. ability to approximate
17. trial and error methods
18. simplifying difficult tasks
19. looking for pattern
20. reasoning
21. making and testing hypotheses
22. proving and disproving

E PERSONAL QUALITIES

23. good working habits
24. positive attitude to maths

Figure 23.2

One helpful way to review the policy is to take an area of maths, say shape or number, and for everyone to work at this aspect of maths. One school took six different maths topics and worked on them for a fortnight each throughout the term, with regular discussions that were therefore focused on the real issues in maths education.

Section C   Practicalities and ways forward

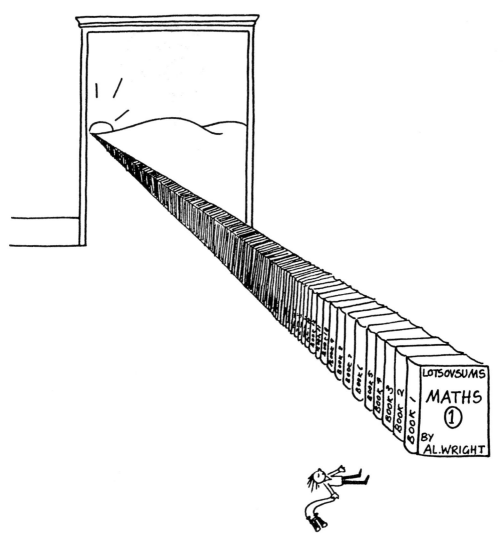

Joy Dunn ©

$-24-$ Starting off
Sue Atkinson

| THEMES: starting points; adult role; discussion starters

In the previous section we have suggested some starting points for maths with reason. For instance, you might like to try 'planning a picnic', p.75; 'building a natural area', p.107; or 'explode a number', p.91. If you work this way, you may have some surprises. This section explores some of the things that might happen.

What can I expect?

- You will not necessarily feel total success first time! You may find it particularly hard learning to stand back and let the children do it.

- Bright children who have been used to getting pages of ticks rather easily, find this more demanding way of working difficult. They are not always the first to 'see' a way to do it and this is hard for them.

- You will need to take care that your interventions are not so heavy that you are telling the children how to do an activity.

- You may well enjoy this approach more and get more from it if you have a parent or a colleague in the room with you.

- Learn to work *with* the children, and try the investigation yourself too. You are the role model for the children; they may be very unsure what you mean by 'investigate it'.

Useful pointers

1 The aim is more to get children to explore possibilities than just to 'get a right answer'.
2 Teachers should try to make the mathematical thinking processes of

maths *explicit to the child*. The different processes are shown in Figure 24.1.

Specialising   Manipulating specific examples to see the underlying pattern and to gain confidence.

Generalising   Once the pattern has been seen, attempts are made to explain it. What is it that is the same about each of the specific examples?

Conjecturing   Verbalising your generalisations. Posing a possible explanation for the pattern.

Verifying   Explaining *why* your conjecture is valid, not just for your special examples, but also in general.

Figure 24.1 Mathematical thinking process

3 Teachers often find some sort of 'rubic' helps them to give some structure to this investigative work (see Figure 24.2). Some teachers put this rubic up on the classroom wall and get the children to refer to it.

STUCK!   It's OK to be stuck – use it as a time to gather your thoughts together.
I KNOW...   What is it that you know?
I WANT...   Where are you trying to go?
TRY...   I've got an idea.
CHECK   Always check everything you do.
REFLECT   What were the 'key moments' in solving the problem?

Figure 24.2 Rubric to help mathematical thinking

- The word 'stuck' is particularly useful. It is much better than saying 'I can't do it.' 'Stuck' is a temporary state and children are encouraged to unstick themselves without the intervention of the teacher. This gives them considerable independence and improves their confidence and self-esteem.
- Children are encouraged when stuck to say what they want and what they already know. Usually it makes the situation clearer to think it through in that framework.
- It makes being 'stuck' part of the normal experience of mathematicians. In classes where this is made a part of the ethos of the class, children do not laugh when a child makes an error. Everyone gets stuck. It's important to show that the teacher gets stuck too!

4 The children should be encouraged to:
- look for pattern;
- say 'What if I... ; 'Would it be the same if ...';
- explore – to 'play with it'; and
- see the 'human sense' in maths – it can be used to solve real problems

5 The children should learn to put their own meanings into their work. Because there isn't a 'right' way, they will more readily apply their intuitive knowledge of maths to the situation.

Investigations and the National Curriculum

It is assumed in the National Curriculum that children will be working on investigations. More than that, though, the whole approach of the National Curriculum is *investigative*.

There is often some confusion between the terms 'investigation' and 'problem solving'. Figure 24.3 illustrates the distinction.

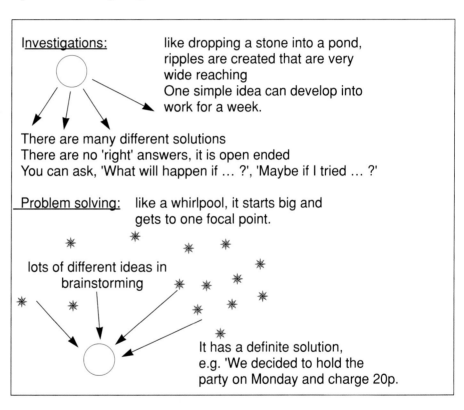

Figure 24.3 Two types of good maths

But the mathematical thinking processes and strategies are the same for both types of maths.

Hints for successful investigations

- Give a choice of investigations whenever possible.

- Give investigations *verbally*, as this tends to help children. The discussion is particularly important when children are new to this way of working.

- It is often a good idea to set aside a whole afternoon for maths activities.

- If you want to start with your whole class, it works well to choose a 'real' problem that everyone will be interested in, e.g. planning a party. If you want to start with an investigation, choose about six investigations of varying types, i.e. spatial, number, puzzles, etc., and read these out to the children as well as having copies that they can come back to later. They can then get into groups, choose an investigation and try it out.

- In the early stages it is important to let children change their minds about what they want to do.

- If you have been used to working in a way where you tell the children exactly what to do, or if you have children who are rather unwilling to think for themselves, be ready for some insecurity to show itself. They *don't know what you are expecting of them* – be patient!

- Investigations where a pattern can be built on the table with Unifix or interlocking cubes can be helpful, as in the making of the patterns you can encourage the children to talk about what they are doing. You can also see who can build the next pattern and who is having difficulty.

- Try to have activities for children to fall back on if interest flags, or you get very involved with one group. I use strategy games 'Ways to win' (p.172), polydrons, interlocking cubes etc. The shape investigations in 'Shape Workshop' (p.173 – one of the Manchester Polytechnic books) fascinate children of any age.

The adult role

- You have an important role to play as *encourager*.
  'That's really good, Jasmin.'
  'What a good idea!'
  'Did you see what Sarah was trying?'

- Keep the atmosphere positive.

- Try not to be 'Big Boss', but silly behaviour needs to be jumped on! Working in this way requires a thoughtful working atmosphere.

- End lessons by sharing ideas. Have a class discussion and let groups explain their work *if they want to*. Do not pressurise. At this early stage – this talking is *a vital parts of maths with reason.*

$-25-$ How can I organise myself?
Sue Atkinson

THEMES classroom organisation; record-keeping; children evaluating

General organisation

- After just a few investigation sessions you will have a great deal of paper! Keeping an investigation folder for each child for loose work is one way that teachers deal with the variety of sizes and types of paper in use. It can go on to the next class and a progression in work can be seen.

- Children can design their own folders. Give them the dimensions of the finished article – to fit into the cupboard, box or tray – discuss what it *must* have, like a clear name, and flaps to keep the work in. They are then challenged to design an envelope by folding. They can use rough paper for a trial design. The finished product could be covered with mathematical designs.

- I use a box to store the folders. This makes it easy for children to put their own work away.

- Put out a choice of investigative work for children to choose from that will move the focus of maths away from a scheme and make it enjoyable and less competitive. This selection of work can also include language tasks like cloze and crosswords, etc.

- Gather together all the maths resources that you can find and split them up into files of the different areas of maths. So, if a child needs more work on, say, area, it is readily available.

- Make maths apparatus easily accessible in the classroom. Label shelves or drawers so that everyone know where everything is kept.

- End lessons with *everyone* tidying *everything* up!

- Reserve a special place to keep any 3-D work. Small classrooms may need to have extra shelves.

- Make a maths investigation board and encourage children to put up their own work, or to use it to pose problems for the rest of the class. This board can include the 'rubric' (shown on p. 152) to help maths thinking.

- Make specific maths displays so that maths is seen as a vitally important part of classroom life.

Planning

TOPIC DATE			
Exposition			
Discussion child/child child/teacher			
Practice and consolidation			
Investigations			
Problem solving			
Games			
Relevant practical			
Maths across curriculum topic			
Technology and information technology			
Mental maths			
Cooperative group work			
Aesthetic pattern design			
Evaluation			

Figure 25.1 Planning chart

- You may find it helpful to use the chart shown in Figure 25.1 to plan work. This shows the elements of a 'balanced diet' in maths, (developed from the Cockroft Report and *Mathematics 5–16*). The chart helps to check that over the term, the children are receiving a balance of teaching.
- The chart can be used for long-term plans, perhaps half a term, and also for weekly/fortnightly plans.

Children evaluate

- Gathering all the children together sitting on the carpet is an important aspect of my maths teaching. These are times to evaluate, to look at the next stage and times when everyone's ideas go into the melting pot – often a time when children will get their own ideas for future work.

- This will only work if there is an ethos in the class of mutual support, where everyone respects everyone else. Saying that you do not understand must provoke the reaction, 'Can I help you?' It must never provoke a laugh or a put-down – a frighteningly common feature of children in the more competitive environment.

- Planning and working on a balanced maths diet in this way, children are very naturally involved in their own evaluations of their work. Using a maths diary is one effective way to do this.

A maths diary

This is simply a notebook, that can replace the traditional squared maths exercise book, in which an entry is put most days by either the child, teacher or parent. I use a diary in combination with a loose-leaf folder as this gives me maximum flexibility. I also make special little books that may reflect class project work or a specific maths topic, for example 'My book of sharing', 'Colour maths', or 'Roman maths'.

Some pages from Alex's maths diary are reproduced here (see Figure 25.2 overleaf). Everyone becomes involved in the maths diary, part-time support teachers, classroom assistants, parents, and the headteacher. Children as well as adults can be encouraged to write evaluative comments, so that the diary has a much wider purpose than just a straightforward maths exercise book.

Record-keeping

Basic day-to-day record-keeping can be focused in a maths diary. In addition to this, your own notes can include jottings of interesting things, gaps in children's understanding, areas covered, and observations etc. I put these notes on a class list on a clipboard, then each half-term or full term, the child's diary and my own notes can be used to write a half-page 'maths profile' of a child for their record folder. These are my comments about Alexander (aged eight):

Alexander has made good progress this half-term. For a few weeks he found it hard to see that '3 groups of 4' did not mean 'a group of 3 and

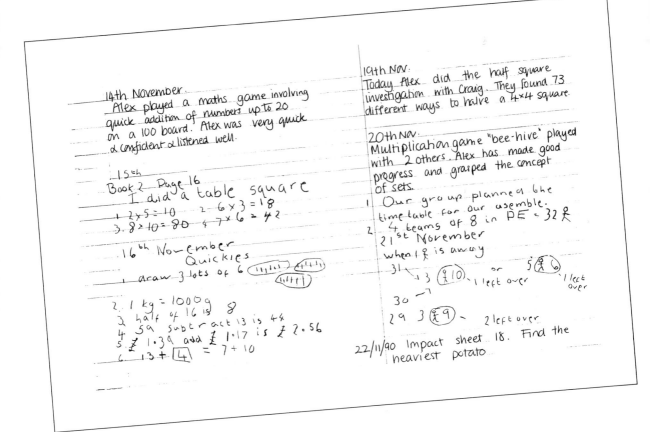

Figure 25.2 Extract from Alex's maths diary

a group of 4', but he has grasped this concept now. He has covered work on multiplication and money, and in IMPACT he has worked on shopping and weighing. He is much more confident these days and willing to discuss his work openly in class. He continues to work well in a group, and understands problems clearly and enjoys solving them.

Alexander's recording of his work is clearer, and he is now more prepared to try things in his own way. He enjoyed the challenge of finding ways to shorthand '3 sets of 4 makes 12 altogether'. He is becoming more systematic in investigative work.

Alexander likes learning tables and his mother is helping him. They have a tables chart for his bedroom wall.

He is becoming increasingly confident with the calculator, and seems to be clear about the '+' and '-' signs. He has learnt the multiplication sign, and calls it 'sets of', or 'times', and uses it well in calculator activities, but this needs consolidating.

Alexander is enjoying his IMPACT sheets, and most have been returned this term. He has a great deal of home support.

The key issues for any record-keeping system are:

- it must be simple and concise;

- you must like the system and develop it for your school or your cluster of schools;

- it must show not only work covered and the level of attainment in National Curriculum terms, such as a simple tick list would show, but it should also show the child's attitude to maths, their confidence etc., as we have discussed throughout this book. (This latter point relates closely to New Attainment Target 1, and to the issues of confidence etc. addressed in this book.)

- it must be clear to parents, readily available to them and include their comments.

Some schools are developing this aspect of maths record-keeping along the lines of Liz Waterland's (1985) circles used for reading (see Figure 25.3a). Other schools are developing similar ideas, but using a brick wall (see Figure 25.3b).

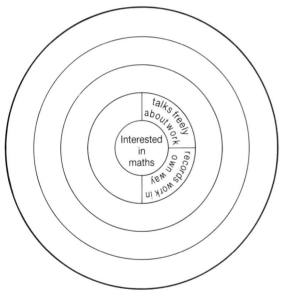

Figure 25.3a Concentric circle record

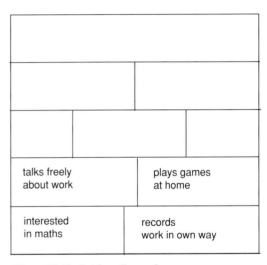

Figure 25.3b Brick wall record

Examples of some of the sections of the circle, or 'bricks' of the wall for reception children might be:

- interested in maths;

- talks freely about work;

- able to record work using own 'writing' and pictures;

- approaches tasks confidently;

- relates 'home' and 'school' maths;

- engages in maths activities at home;
- able to 'see' and describe a simple sequential pattern;
- uses own symbols for words;
- uses own symbols for numbers;
- uses standard symbols for numbers;
- uses a calculator;
- understands addition with small numbers;
- understands subtraction with small numbers.

Many of these would clearly be appropriate at later stages also.

—26— How do I develop my confidence?

THEMES maths panic: maths from picture books; parents and teachers working together; discussion starters

Parents and teachers working together

1 Talk about the 'blob tree' (see Figure 26.1 overleaf). Who can you identify with when it comes to maths? Sometimes this helps people to identify their feelings about maths.

Do feel you are falling off! Do you just need someone alongside you? (Not everyone may want to share their feelings in a group, of course.)

2 Discuss Figure 26.2 – 'Panic about maths'.

3 Have a special maths games/activity time once a week – perhaps Friday afternoon while all the tidying up is going on.

4 Look at your needs together and decide on priorities. Is the class so big that help is needed in small groups? Does the water-play need an adult there to do some language development? Do the bright ones need some special help? Do you need more storage space?

5 Think of starting some simple home/school maths games or worksheets, see p. 147. Start small, then review it.

6 Could the PTA raise money for some special maths or technology/construction equipment?

7 Many schools have invested time and money in making maths games and this has proved an excellent source of confidence boosting for both children and adults.

Figure 26.1 The 'blob tree'
(Reproduced from Games Without Frontiers *with the kind permission of Pip Wilson, this book, published by Marshall Pickering, contains other group ice-breakers and ideas from getting groups thinking. The book is available by post from Romford YMCA, Rush Green Road, Romford RM7 0PH.)*

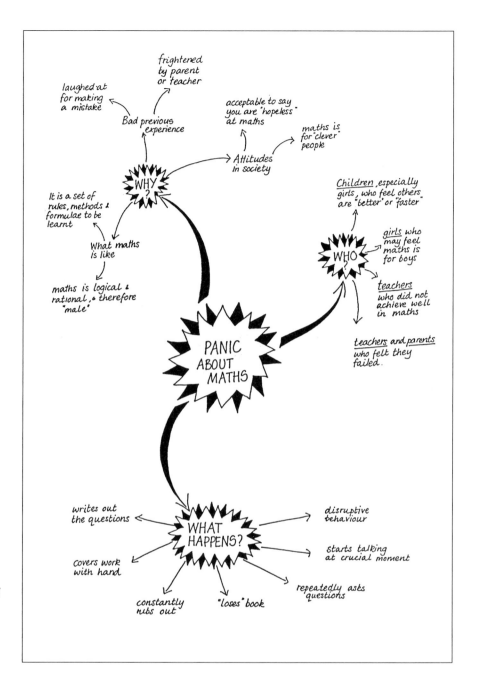

Figure 26.2 Panic about maths
© Sue Atkinson and
Joy Dunn
(developed from
'Genderwatch'
SCDC)

For teachers

1 Try out one of the ideas from the teachers' stories in Section B.

2 Observe what is already going on. Where are your real needs?

3 If you find it too threatening to have parents in the room while you do maths (and for lots of teachers this is the case) then think how you could involve parents to benefit the children.

4 Building up your knowledge will help you to feel more confident. There are two aspects to this:

(a) Good classroom resources for ideas and starting points.

(b) In the long-term you will need to build up your 'craft knowledge' of what you are doing in maths and about the processes of mathematical thinking.

There are some very good and easy to understand packs and courses available and these are listed on p. 173.

5 Ask someone to work with you. It does not have to be someone confident with maths, just someone who is willing to work alongside you and support you as you try to improve your practice.

For parents

1 Do a mathematical activity with your child where you feel confident like cooking, gardening or DIY. Think how you could develop this activity. Does she need more help with reading weighing scales, or with measuring distances? Could you find recipes, or some gardening that he could do entirely on his own?

2 Build up a collection of mathematical games. Plan to play them two or three times a week – rather like the way you help with reading.

3 Don't focus on 'sums'! Try to broaden your child's view of maths and boost his confidence.

4 Give out a positive aura. Don't say 'I was no good at maths so I don't suppose you will be either'!

5 Get a good book to help you.

6 Ask your child's teachers what you can do to help. Tell them you do not feel very confident! They probably don't either!

7 Be aware of the mathematical possibilities in story books. Once you start to see them, you will be hooked!

Of course, the child entering into the magic of the book is the crucial thing, but at the end, as well as discussing the story, try to think of the mathematical aspects. Most picture books have considerable mathematical content. Don't just count things, but think of all the position, measuring and quantity words that your child needs for maths, for example, 'between', 'through', 'under', 'around', 'heavy', 'more than', in', 'out of', 'grew', 'enough', 'became smaller', 'late', as well as words for probability, such as 'probably', 'might happen', 'chance', and 'impossible'.

Here are a few examples of questions you could use after reading *Dogger* by Shirley Hughes.

Where do you think Dogger was when he was lost?

Do you think Dave thought he had a good chance of finding Dogger again?

How much are the hats at the fête?

Many familiar stories are good for sequencing events – a vital skill for secure maths understanding: *The House That Jack Built*, *The Enormous Turnip*, and *Jack And The Beanstalk*.

Some quotes from parents

'I panic about maths. As I am talking to you now my heart is pounding. I had to learn lots of the formulae for exams just when I was going through adolescent traumas, and I just couldn't cope. Now, if maths is mentioned, I go all hot and cold. I cannot help my own children, because I panic as soon as they tell me the problem. I want them to understand, not just be told to learn it by rote... Most of all, I don't want them to panic like I did.'

'I coped with maths quite well until I was eleven and went to Grammar School, and then it was all xs and ys, and I didn't know what they were talking about.'

'I wasn't any good at maths, so I don't suppose my child will be either.'

'They do things like cooking at school, and lots of practical maths, but now she is seven, I want her to get on with some real maths.'

'I don't want my child to suffer what I went through. I want her to enjoy it and understand it.'

'You're failing my child. She is four, in the nursery, and she doesn't know her tables yet.'

'My child needs *more* arithmetic, *more* straight computation. That's what I failed on. I just couldn't do it and I am conscious that I failed at it. I don't want that to happen to my child... I don't approve of all this messing about with shapes and cubes.'

(*To a teacher doing home/school maths project*) 'We loved it, we all did it together, it was great fun. My husband and I agreed that the maths we had done as children was boring. This was great fun and Mark learnt a lot. Please could we have some more tonight?'

(*Mother of a six-year-old child*) '... but they ought to be learning their tables. I go into help some days, and they ask me to play maths games. I quite enjoy doing that and the children love it, but it is not real maths, is it?'

'I couldn't believe it. Daren, aged five, said to me, "Mum, twenty point five is half of forty-one, so we get twenty and a half sweets each." He worked it out on a calculator... he brings it to the supermarket and adds up the shopping. And he gets it right, which is more than I can do – I keep pressing the wrong buttons.'

(*Mother of children aged eight, six and four*) 'We love the maths games that we borrowed from school. We get one each week and the kids are really keen on maths now. I hope they never hate it like I did.'

−27− Asking ourselves questions
Marion Bird

| THEMES questions for teachers; professional development;
discussion starters

In this section, Marion Bird asks some questions that we will always need to go on asking ourselves. There is always more for us to learn when we are dealing with young children – that's what makes it so exciting! By keeping these questions in our mind we make maths a time of exploration for us, as well as for the children.

Through these questions I am trying to capture the essence of some of the thinking which I feel lies behind my on-going actions and reactions when working with children.

- How can the children be encouraged to carry out mathematical activities themselves rather than merely to learn the results of someone else's mathematical thinking? By 'mathematical activities' here, I mean such activities as searching for patterns, setting patterns, making conjectures, testing conjectures, generalising, asking 'why?', trying to be systematic, classifying, transforming, searching for methods, deciding on rules, defining, agreeing on equivalences, reasoning, demonstrating, proving.

- How can the children also be encouraged to ask their own questions, make their own suggestions and choose which ideas to pursue?
  What possibilities for development are embedded in what the children are doing/observing? How can I involve the children in seeing these for themselves?

- Is the starting point accessible to all the children?
  Is it something which is likely to throw up other ideas?
  How can I phrase the initial invitation-to-explore so that it is meaningful to the children and something with which they can immediately engage?

- How can I avoid becoming involved in explaining?
  How can I seek to stop myself intervening when such interventions are likely to end up disturbing unconstructively or taking away potential for initiatives from the children?
  How can I stop myself from exhausting a situation in front of the children?

- How can I slot in terms and notations so that meaning can readily be ascribed to them? ... so that they can be seen as helpful? ... necessary?
  How might the pupils be encouraged to find their own ways of expressing their findings and questions?
  How might the pupils be encouraged to decide on their own terms and notations?
  How can I stop myself simply asking children to 'write it down'? How might they be encouraged to feel a need to write or talk?
  How can I seek to make fruitful use of any scope for pupils to be involved in interpreting what others say and record?
  Can any comments about the importance of being careful how thoughts and calculations are recorded come up as a result of children actually experiencing the importance themselves? (For example, because they have misread something they wrote earlier.)

- If pupils find that something they thought would continue to work actually breaks down, how might I focus on this constructively?
  How can I stop myself indicating to them that something will not work before they have perceived that that is the case?

- How can I try to ensure that their convictions have come about through their own thinking and actions and not just through believing me?

- How can I stop myself passing on any idea that a particular method is to be used? If a variety of methods/strategies are being used, how might I draw attention constructively to these?

- If discrepancies or difficulties arise, can the children be encouraged to work at these and sort them out themselves?
  How might the children be encouraged to check what they are doing for themselves?

- How can I encourage the children to seek connections?

- Suppose I want to make a point about something. Can I use what a child has done to help make the point so that it does not appear as merely my idea?

- Is there scope to draw attention to the distinction between 'It is impossible because I have not found a way' and 'It is impossible because there is no way to be found'?

- If a child comes up with something which appears to me as off the track for the moment, can I stop myself from immediately implying that that is so and ask myself whether in fact it is so? What about the possibility of it being kept as a 'further idea' for later?

- Is working at the arithmetic itself getting in the way? Might using calculators help?

- Are any children perceiving constraints which I did not intend? How might I try to involve them in relaxing these?

$-28-$ Conclusions

We have seen how children need maths to be set in meaningful situations, with experience rooted in the manipulation of appropriate apparatus, and the opportunity to talk to each other and to adults.

Where these conditions for mathematical learning are not given, the children will tend to develop their own meanings and 'tricks' for mathematical work, which are often based on misunderstandings. At its worst, maths can become meaningless gibberish.

There is probably no one right way to teach maths, but one of the central features in the craft of teaching seems to be creating real-life situations in which children can apply their own intuitive meanings and learn to self-correct and check their own meanings against what they have learnt in the new situation.

In this learning, language and activity play vital roles. We have seen the importance of demystifying maths, and making it accessible to children by encouraging the use of their own symbols and recording, and focusing on the language and contexts that they already understand. Within these meaningful contexts, panic is much less likely to arise. Maths does not become an area of fear and mystery but is seen as a useful and relevant part of life.

As Martin Hughes points out, children come to school with far more mathematical ability than we often recognise, and we have seen how parents and teachers can build on this intuitive 'home' learning and language.

When we set maths in contexts that make 'human sense', and we allow children to use their own symbols, and to develop their own meanings, we are respecting their view of the world: 'This is what I think, Amy. What do you think?'

It is exploration together – co-working – that holds the essence of good educational practice. The minute we treat children as empty vessels with buckets of knowledge to be poured into them, we lose that excitement of exploration. Of course, there needs to be a curriculum. We cannot wander aimlessly around in human knowledge. And as the child gets older, there is an increasing need to learn facts and for exposition from the teacher.

Effective teaching unleashes the power of the children's own thinking, their use of symbols, language, and ideas. Creative teaching harnesses all that into the constructed curriculum and, as we show in this book, teaching 'maths with reason' also means that children can function exceptionally well in National Curriculum terms.

Ideally, adults try to give children experiences which make the skills of maths secure, where children have to apply their knowledge in depth until they develop a firm 'brick wall' of knowledge, with a foundation based on confidence and understanding. They come to school as potential mathematicians, and 'maths with reason' helps this potential to emerge.

Repeatedly, teachers are finding that they can give children these types of experiences with maths with reason. Children seem to perform well in complex and unfamiliar mathematical settings, provided, as in any task, they are given the time and space to see the meaning in what they are doing. These teachers view with alarm a 'back to basics' approach to maths, simply returning to the old method of repeated practice. They believe that this will not necessarily reduce the deficiencies that show up at present in maths attainment. Repeated practice of basic skills does not lead to the highest standards. Maths set in meaningful contexts does.

English/American vocabulary sheet

'Have tea' – to have a late afternoon snack.

'VAT' – value added tax, a government tax added when buying some items.

'Squash' and 'concentrate' – two words for a liquid concentrated fruit drink made up with water.

Unifix – plastic multi-purpose counting cubes and associated manipulatives.

Chips – French fries.

Open University – a university that is open to all where study is done at home through distance learning materials. Many teachers take these courses for professional development.

First School – a school that children would go to from age 5 until either 8 or 9.

Primary school – any school with children up to age 13.

Dienes – multibase manipulatives used to teach place value.

Nappies – diapers.

Crisps – potato chips.

Other Terms

CAN project – the Calculator Aware Number project. Part of the PrIME project that looked specifically at what happens when children of 5 – 7 are given calculators right from the start of their schooling.

PrIME project – the Primary Initiatives in Mathematics Education, a British three year project undertaken by teachers and educationalists to look at all aspects of teaching on the mathematics curriculum for children up to age 13.

ILEA – the Inner London Education Authority (now disbanded).

Colour factor rods and Cuisenaire rods – wooden rods used to teach number concepts.

Developmental writing – writing in which children are encouraged to make up their own spelling, (or even symbols in very young children). This book has been explored widely in Britain with remarkable results in both the quantity and the quality of children's writing.

Reception class – the class that a 4 or 5 year old would go into when they first come to school, or after Nursery school. It is almost equivalent to a kindergarten class.

Biscuits – cookies.

Supply teacher – substitute teacher.

Maths scheme – these are schemes of work published by various companies that claim to provide a complete and comprehensive curriculum for children. They are often made up of work cards, work sheets and text books that many teachers use for the children to work with on an individual basis.

Reading books – basal readers.

National Curriculum – a curriculum laid down by the British government that must be taught in all state (public) schools.

Attainment Targets – parts of the National Curriculum that children will be assessed on, eg. in the maths curriculum there are 5 ATs, algebra, number, shape and space, using and applying maths and use of data.

Resources

Books for parents and teachers

How Children Learn Mathematics by P. Liebeck (1984). Harmondsworth: Penguin.
Maths through Play by R. Griffiths (1988). London: Macdonald.
A Parent's Guide to Your Child's Maths by R. Merttens (1988): London Octopus. (There are many books in the Parent and Child Programme, published by Octopus books and available in high street shops.)
Help Your Child with Maths by A. Walsh (1988). London: BBC.

Resources for games

Angela Walsh's book, as above.
Make games resource book, from NARE, 2, Lichfield Road, Stafford ST17 4JX. (An economical starter).
Design a Board Game. Longman. (Great for age 7 and above.)
Count me in. HBJ Maths, Foots Cray High Street, Sidcup, Kent DA14 5HP. (A set of games – send for the brochure.)
Song books:
This Little Puffin compiled by E. Matterson (1969). Harmondsworth, Penguin
Count Me In (1984) A & C Black.
Ways to Win, Strategy games. Manchester Polytechnic books. See opposite page. (A brilliant and economical book of strategy games.)

Home–school maths

Any of the other resources mentioned.

Ruth Merttens book as stated previously, or send for the IMPACT starter pack, Polytechnic of North London, Holloway Road, London, N7 8DB.

Resources for maths in the classroom

Tarquin and Dime Publications, Stradbroke, Diss, Norfolk IP21 5JP. (Lots of creative ideas, games, posters, activities etc. In a class of its own)

Many useful resources e.g. *Sharing Mathematics with Parents* by S. Thornes, and various books by Marion Bird can be obtained from the Mathematical Association, 259 London Road, Leicester, LE2 3BE.

ATM, 7 Shaftsbury Street, Derby, DE3 8YB. (Mostly books for teachers.)

The Mathematics Centre, West Sussex Institute of Higher Education, Upper Bognor Road, Bognor Regis, West Sussex, PO21 1HR.

Claire Publications, York House, Bacons Lane, Chappel, Colchester, Essex, CO6 2EB. (Good quality photocopiable resources produced by teachers.)

Triad Publications, 15 St. Peter's Court, Hospital Road, Bury St. Edmunds, Suffolk, IP33 3LY. (Produced by teachers for teachers; some unusual starting points and photocopiable.)

Books by Sue Atkinson on photocopiable classroom activities, e.g., probability, place value etc. can be obtained from Philip and Tacey Ltd., North Way, Andover, Hants SO10 5BA.

Manchester Polytechnic books. Gillian Hatch, Manchester Polytechnic, Didsbury Site, 799 Wilmslow Road, Didsbury, Manchester M20 8RR. (Don't be without these resources. Produced by teachers. The cheapest books of their kind. *Bounce to It* is an outstanding collection of investigations for 5–7 year olds.)

Resources for Learning and Development Unit, Bishop Road, Bishopston, Bristol BS7 8LS. List of products and prices on request. Particularly recommended: *Piers is Lost*.

Maths on Display: creative ideas for the teaching of infant maths by B. Hume and K. Barrs, Belair.

Nuffield Maths Teacher's Handbooks. Longman. (Get the book that relates to the age of the child you are teaching. It is full of activities for teaching particular concepts.)

Primary Mathematics Today by E. Williams and H. Shuard (3rd edition). Longman.

Maths in-service

Supporting Primary Mathematics – A pack to support maths and the National Curriculum. Open University.

Maths in the National Curriculum. A course unit in the modular Primary Profile, Open University. For details of both of these, and other Open University materials, write to: The Centre for Maths Education, Open University, Walton Hall, Milton Keynes MK7 6AA.

Children, Mathematics and Learning, produced by the PrIME team, Hilary Shuard *et al.*, Simon and Schuster.

Games without Frontiers by Pip Wilson. Starters for groups of adults or young people. Available from: Romford YMCA, Rush Green Road., Romford RM7 0PH.

Resources in North America

Didax, 1 Centennial Drive, Centennial Industrial Park, Peabody, MA 01960 (Comprehensive general resources, manipulatives etc. including the wonderful Unifix cube.)

Zephyr Press, 3316 N. Chapel Ave., PO Box 13448-C, Dept., Tucson, Arizona 85732 – 3448. (Mostly good quality books for teachers.)

Good Apple, 1204 Buchanan St., PO Box 299, Carthage IL. 62321 – 0299. (Produced by teachers for teachers.)

Creative Publications, 5040 West 111th Street, Oak Lawn, IL 60453. (As its name suggests, these are creative ideas for teaching maths; books, manipulatives etc. These are distributed in Britain by Jonathan Press, York House, Bacons Lane, Chappel, Colchester, Essex. CO6 2EB.)

References

ASSESSMENT OF PERFORMANCE UNIT (1980) Mathematical Development. Primary Survey Report No. 1. London: HMSO.

BERENSTAIN, S. and BERENSTAIN, J. (1972) *Bears in the Night*. Glasgow: Collins.

BIRD, M. (1991) *Mathematics for Young Children*. London: Routledge.

BRISSENDEN, T. (1988) *Talking about Mathematics: Mathematical Discussion in Primary Classrooms*. Oxford: Basil Blackwell.

BRUCE, T. *Early Childhood Education* (1987). London: Hodder and Stoughton.

BRUNER, J.S. (1984) *Beyond the Information Given*. London: Allen and Unwin.

BUXTON, L.G. (1981) *Do You Panic about Maths? Coping with Maths Anxiety*. London: Heinemann.

BUXTON, L.G. (1982) Emotional Response to Symbolism, *Visible Language*, **xvi**, **3**, 215–20.

CAN (Calculator Aware Numbers) Project. Part of the PrIME project, Shuard, H. (ed.) 1991. London. Simon and Schuster.

CLAY, M. (1975) *What did I write?* London: Heinemann.

DEPARTMENT OF EDUCATION AND SCIENCE (1967) *Children and their Primary Schools* (Plowden Report). London: HMSO.

DEPARTMENT OF EDUCATION AND SCIENCE (1978) *Primary Education in England* (HMI Report). London: HMSO.

DEPARTMENT OF EDUCATION AND SCIENCE (1982) *Mathematics Counts.* (Cockroft Report). HMSO.

DEPARTMENT OF EDUCATION AND SCIENCE (1985) *Mathematics from 5–16, Curriculum Matters 3.* London: HMSO.

DONALDSON, M. (1978) *Children's Minds.* London: Fontana.

DONALDSON, M., GRIEVE, R. and PRATT, C. (eds.), (1983) *Early Childhood Education.* Oxford: Basil Blackwell.

DUFOUR-JANVIER, B. et al. (1987) Pedagogical considerations concerning the problem of representation, in JANVIER, C. (ed.), *Problems of representation in the teaching and learning of Mathematics.* New Jersey, USA.

FLETCHER, H. (1979) *Mathematics in Schools.* London: Addison Wesley.

FLOYD, A. (ed.) (1981) *Developing Mathematical Thinking.* London: Open University/Addison Wesley.

GELMAN, R. and GALLISTEL, C.R. (1978) *The Child's Understanding of Number.* Cambridge, Mass: Harvard University Press.

GINSBURG, H.P. (1977) *Children's Arithmetic: the Learning Process.* New York: Van Nostrand.

GRAVES, D. (1983) *Writing: Teachers and children at work.* London: Heinemann.

GROEN, G. and RESNICK, L.B. (1977) Can pre-school children invent addition algorithms? *Journal of Educational Psychology,* **69**, 645–52.

HALL, N. (1989) *Writing with Reason.* London: Hodder and Stoughton.

HART, K.M. (ed.) (1981) *Children's Understanding of Mathematics: 11–16.* London: John Murray.

HUGHES, M. (1986a) Bridge that Gap, *Child Education.* **63**, **2** p. 13–15 and **63**, **3** p. 13–15. London: Scholastic.

HUGHES, M. (1986b) *Children and Number: Difficulties in Learning Mathematics.* Oxford: Basil Blackwell.

HUGHES, S. (1977) *Dogger.* London: The Bodley Head.

JAMES, N. and MCCARTNEY, R. (1987) *E802 Applied Studies in Mathematical Education.* Milton Keynes: Open University Press.

JAMES, N. and MASON, J. (1982) Towards Recording, *Visible Language*, XVI, 249–58.

MCGARRIGLE, J., GRIEVE, R. and HUGHES, M. (1978) Interpreting inclusion: a contribution to the study of the child's cognitive and linguistic development. *Journal of Experimental Child Psychology*. **26**, 528–550.

MASON, J. et al. (1982) *Thinking Mathematically*. London: Addison Wesley.

NATIONAL ASSESSMENT OF EDUCATIONAL PROGRESS (1983) *The Third National Mathematics Assessment: Results, trends and issues*. Denver: Education Commission of the States.

NATIONAL CURRICULUM COUNCIL (1989) *Mathematics in the National Curriculum*. London: HMSO.

OPEN UNIVERSITY (1980) Course PME 233; *Mathematics Across the Curriculum*. Milton Keynes: Open University Press.

OPEN UNIVERSITY (1982) Course EM 235. *Developing Mathematical thinking*. Milton Keynes: Open University Press.

PIAGET, J. (1953) *The Child's Conception of Number*. London: Routledge and Kegan Paul.

SCDC (1989) *Becoming a Writer* (National Writing Project). Thomas Nelson & Son Ltd. London.

SHUARD, H. and ROTHERAY, A. (eds.) (1984) *Children Reading Mathematics*. London: Murray.

SHUARD, H. (1986) *Primary Mathematics Today and Tomorrow*. York: Longman.

SKEMP. R.R. (1976) Relational Understanding and Instrumental Understanding, *Mathematics Teaching 77*, 20–6.

SKEMP, R.R. (1982) Communicating Mathematics: Surface Structures and Deep Structures, *Visible Language **XVI** 3*, 281–288.

SKEMP, R.R. (1986) *Primary Mathematics Project for the Intelligent Learning of Mathematics*. Department of Education, University of Warwick.

TIZARD, B. and HUGHES, M. (1984) *Young Children Learning*. London: Fontana.

VYGOTSKI, L. (1978) *Mind in Society*. Cambridge, Mass: Harvard University Press.

VYGOTSKI, L. (1983) School instruction and mental development, in DONALDSON, M., GRIEVE, R., and PRATT, C. (eds.) *Early Childhood Development and Education*. Oxford: Basil Blackwell.

WATERLAND, L. (1985) *Read with Me. An Apprenticeship Approach to Reading*. South Woodchester, Stroud: Thimble Press.

WATERLAND, L. (ed.) (1989) *Apprenticeship in Action: Teachers Write about Read with Me*. South Woodchester, Stroud: Thimble Press.

WELLS, G. and NICHOLLS, J. (eds.) (1985) *Language and Learning: An Interactional Perspective*. London: Falmer Press.

WINNICOTT, D.W. (1971) *Playing and Reality*. London: Tavistock Publications. Also (1984) Harmondsworth: Penguin Books.